BST 3/19/08

ACPL ITEM

DISCA

3 1833 053

Y0-BTD-536

How to Col ~~~~~~~ Dollars
for Reporting Fraud

WHISTLE BLOWING

A Guide to Government Reward Programs

JOEL D. HESCH, ESQ.

Copyright © 2008 by Joel D. Hesch, Esq.

All rights reserved. No part of this book may be reproduced in any form or by any electronic or mechanical means without permission in writing from the publisher and author, except by a reviewer, who may quote brief passages in a review.

Published and printed in the United States of America

First edition

ISBN:
978-0-9772602-0-1
0-9772602-0-8

Business/Money/Finance

LCCN: 2007903312

Goshen Press
3540 Ridgecroft Dr.
Lynchburg, VA 24503

Disclaimers. The views expressed by the author are his own personal beliefs and do not represent the views of the Department of Justice (DOJ) or Liberty University School of Law, where the author is a professor.

Although some of this book is based in part upon true cases, the names and facts have been altered in order to best illustrate points to aid in your understanding of the government reward programs. Therefore, even if you think you recognize a case used as an illustration, it is not intended to represent a particular case.

This book should not be construed as legal advice. Each case is unique and must be evaluated on its own merits. Past amounts of recoveries do not guarantee future rewards. You should consult an attorney experienced with the Department of Justice Reward Program, before deciding whether to file for a reward.

Publisher's Cataloging-in-Publication
(Provided by Quality Books, Inc.)

Hesch, Joel D.
   Whistleblowing : a guide to government reward
programs (how to collect millions of dollars for
reporting fraud) / by Joel D. Hesch. — 1st ed.
      p. cm.
      Includes index.
      LCCN 2007903312
      ISBN-13: 978-0-9772602-0-1
      ISBN-10: 0-9772602-0-8

   1. Whistle blowing. 2. Fraud—United States.
3. United States—Claims. 4. Public contracts—United
States. 5. Popular actions—United States.   I. Title.

JF1525.W45H47 2007   353.4'6
                    QBI07-700140

Contents

Introduction

*Let us have faith that right makes might, and in that faith,
let us, to the end, dare to do our duty as we understand it.*

— Abraham Lincoln

In the movie *Erin Brockovich,* actress Julia Roberts plays a devoted-mom-turned-whistleblower after discovering that residents of a small town have an abnormal rate of cancer. After doing some digging, she discovers that a large power plant is contaminating the local water. Incensed, she begins a crusade to hold the company accountable.

Driven by the need for justice, Erin Brockovich cannot be stopped. This gutsy woman single-handedly takes on the goliath company, which tries to block her at every turn. Because of her doggedness, truth and justice ultimately prevail. The company agrees to change its hazardous waste disposal and to pay $300 million in damages.

Hollywood does a wonderful job of presenting this story as a heart-racing, action adventure, as the whistleblower risks life and limb to protect innocent lives. Other movies have depicted the heroic acts of whistleblowers as well. Often based on true stories, Hollywood films have repeatedly shown ordinary citizens, stepping up bravely to save lives. In *The Insider,* Russell Crowe portrayed a whistleblower acting on his sense of outrage to save people from the clutches of tobacco firms that were placing addictive agents in their products and bringing to light the falsified studies that had been used to gain FDA approval of dangerous drugs.

In movies, a whistleblower is often a lone maverick, who acts on passionate convictions and endures severe retaliation (or even death) at the hand of the powers they dare to report. Their only reward is the satisfaction that they did the right thing. Although this heightened danger and against-all-odds determination makes for great drama, the reality is, the characters in these stories don't bear much resemblance to the new breed of 21st-century whistleblowers.

For one thing, there's no longer any need to be a maverick with an obsession, willing to risk everything in the name of justice. Government agencies, such as the Department of Justice (DOJ), the Internal Revenue Service (IRS), and many state departments actively court citizens to join in the fight against fraud. While not every kind of illegal fraud is covered by these programs, most fraud that costs the government a substantial amount of money, under government programs or contracts, and underpayment of taxes, are eligible for rewards.

The government has taken two steps lay out a warm welcome mat to encourage you to step forward and report fraud:

1. Huge monetary rewards (often in the millions)
2. Increased protection against retaliation against whistleblowers.

The large money rewards have legitimized modern-day whistleblowers. The government has forged an important alliance with the public — one it constantly fosters. Similarly, the new antiretaliation provisions are not meaningless additions to the program. They contain rows of sharp teeth, including double damages and attorney fees, which act as both an effective deterrence and as valuable restitution for violations. There is no longer a feeling that whistleblowers must go into hiding for being willing to step forward and do the right thing.

This book is designed to broadcast the existence of three powerful government programs that allow you to partner with the government, report fraud, see justice done, and collect a sizeable reward.

As a former DOJ Attorney, I will give you a personal tour of these exciting reward programs. In plain English, I make clear the technical rules, provide you with checklists to start testing your case, and warn you of pitfalls to avoid. You will be better able discern whether you have a case worth pursuing.

Every year, DOJ pays hundreds of millions of dollars in rewards. I worked on many of these cases and am describing the common fraud schemes DOJ has vigorously pursued and paid huge monetary rewards. That allows you to study many of the fraud schemes and cases presented in this book to see exactly what's involved.

As you get to know the DOJ program, you will see that the state and IRS programs are virtually identical to this program. That makes it easier for you to apply for rewards in all three programs!

The second section of this book addresses the growing number of state reward programs. Due to the huge success of the federal reward program, at least a dozen states have created their own reward programs. More and more states are proposing similar statutes. In the next few years, virtually all of the remaining states are expected to adopt reward programs. The opportunities to collect rewards are growing every day.

In the last section of the book, you'll learn about the new IRS Reward Program. In December 2006, the IRS totally revamped its little-used reward program and modeled it after the highly successful DOJ Reward Program.

It was almost unthinkable a few years back, but now the government has agreed to pay up to 30 percent of the amount the IRS recovers from tax cheaters. As I write this, the IRS is in the process of forming a whistleblower office in Washington, D.C. and placing a welcome mat at its front door for you. This book not only describes the new program, but adds checklists for you to follow in making an assessment of your case.

This is your definitive guidebook. No step will be left out — from the moment you suspect fraud, until the day the government recovers the funds and pays your reward!

Real Help

Although the reward programs are complex, you won't find legalese in this book. In simple terms you'll be walked through the entire process from the time you are just wondering whether you have a good case to actually receiving a reward. You'll also be introduced to the types of fraud cases the government has historically accepted as well as rejected. Through vivid examples, you will get a glimpse of the myriad of ways fraud is committed. The goal is aiding you in spotting a fraud case and then knowing how to properly report it and apply for a reward.

Significant time and detail are devoted to major policies and procedures. In Chapter Six, I distill the model DOJ program into what I coin as the *"Four F Factors."* These are the key features that must be met in order to receive a reward. You'll get a firm grasp of what it takes to satisfy each element. On the flip side, there are pitfalls to avoid. Knowing what they are in advance can help you decide whether you can step over these hurdles or keep you from wasting your time if you cannot.

Virtually every would-be whistleblower wants to get an idea of how much of a reward they might receive. That is why I explain the seemingly secret manner in which DOJ determines the amount of a reward. An entire chapter is devoted to this topic, describing the ranges and factors dictating where a case likely falls. Although you won't be able to predict your reward from reading a book, you'll have a healthy appreciation for how the process works.

CHAPTER ONE

Overview of Government Reward Programs

The biggest reward for a thing well done is to have done it.
— FRANCOIS VOLTAIRE (1694–1778)

Amazingly enough, most Americans are still unaware of these gutsy reward programs. If they realized how rewarding it could be, they'd find it very exciting.

The fact is, one in five whistleblowers who applied received a reward. Even more incredible, one in 25 applicants became a millionaire!

A quarter of a billion dollars in rewards are paid each year, and the amounts are growing. By following this guidebook, you can take steps towards making a substantial portion of that reward money your own.

The government is doing everything in its power to make the program appealing and effective for whistleblowers, because, experience has shown that whistleblowers and the government make an ideal team for fighting fraud.

The modern whistleblower does not fight the battle alone, but links up with government investigators and attorneys dedicated to ferreting out fraud. The days of a whistleblower being a lone wolf are long past. So too are the movie stereotypes where the heroes fear for their lives and end up being chased by hit men.

Today, the largest role of whistleblowers is to put officials on the trail of fraud; allowing them to use the weight of government resources to prove fraud and recover overpayments.

Wouldn't you like to join the fight against companies cheating under military contracts, Medicare, Homeland Security, just to name a few?

Virtually every government program has its share of people who think that government funds are like Monopoly® money or that the public treasury is so deep that a little fraud doesn't matter. The money they take comes out of your pocket, as a faithful taxpayer. Are you willing to put up with that or do you want to do something about it?

Countless numbers of people cheat on taxes every year. Are you willing to stand against that practice? When they take precious resources from the government, existing government programs are less able to work properly. In addition, for every extra dollar needed to replace ones taken by fraud, one more deserving program (such as medical research, education, or even basic road work) either goes unfunded or your taxes are increased to cover the loss.

It's time to put an end to fraudulent claims to the government and cheating on taxes! These reward programs are designed to give you an opportunity to participate.

A New Breed of Whistleblowers

In 1986, the Department of Justice overhauled the DOJ Reward Program to make it more appealing to potential whistleblowers, offering them up to 30 percent of the money recovered. The results were staggering.

Today, a true partnership is being forged between the government and the public to stamp out cheaters who drain precious government funds and cost taxpayers money.

The revised DOJ Reward Program kicked off the new era of modern-day whistleblowers (aka "relators" or one who relates the fraud to the government).

You will soon see why the DOJ Reward Program is the federal government's most effective antifraud tool. It accomplishes several things. First, it allows the government to collect back *three times* the amount of the funds wrongfully paid, as well as significant civil penalties. Second, it invites the public to collect a reward in cases they report.

Further, DOJ allows whistleblowers and their attorneys to stay involved in the process to ensure that cheaters repay all of the ill-gotten gains. Finally, the laws prohibit retaliation against whistleblowers, imposing huge penalties if it is attempted.

The entire tenor of reporting fraud against the government has changed. Citizens are encouraged to join together with special fraud units to combat fraud and receive a portion of the government's recovery, as a way of saying thank you.

The government has a completely new strategy and role for whistleblowers.

First, the DOJ Reward Program is intentionally designed to pay out *extremely large* rewards.

Why? Because paying a whistleblower tens of millions of dollars for doing the right thing in reporting fraud is a headline grabber! Such large rewards act as incentives to draw others forward in reporting fraud. Large rewards also make a company think twice about cheating in the first place. In theory, the fear that one's own employee can earn millions of dollars for reporting misconduct should slow down the amount of fraud in the first place. It also helps to recover from those that still choose to cheat.

You might be wondering whether paying average rewards of close to $2 million really helps government programs? It is simple math.

Congress and others estimate that as much as ten percent of all bills turned into the government are inflated. If this estimate is correct, it means the government currently spends as much as $100 billion a year in fraudulent payments.

Currently, DOJ is recovering over $1 billion a year from companies that have cheated. While this is excellent progress, the difference between $1 billion and $100 billion is a substantial gap!

What can be done about it? Congress decided to pay for help. When it authorized DOJ to pay rewards of up to 30 percent, it was effectively offering to hire you to help it track down the fraud.

You don't have to bring wrongdoers all the way to justice. Whistle-blowers are rewarded handsomely for putting the government on the trail of fraud. There are rules you must follow to qualify. Certain requirements must be met. But this book will guide you through that process.

It is a win-win situation because you stand to make millions of dollars for your careful efforts and the government stands to regain more money than they would have made without you.

So far, the DOJ Reward Program has brought the government $11 billion it may not have tracked down otherwise. It paid whistle-blower rewards of $1.8 billion, which left $9.2 billion net. Not bad for the whistleblowers and not a bad return on investment for the government either.

Snapshot of the DOJ Reward Program

In a case involved a large chain of hospitals, committing systematic fraud, DOJ rewarded a whistleblower with $100 million. Of course, the whistleblowers had seasoned legal counsel on their team who were familiar with the complexities of the DOJ Reward Program.

In every case, it is vital that you enlist an attorney familiar with the DOJ Reward Program who can help you shape the application in a way that will jumpstart the government investigation. Those who try to make the application without experienced legal counsel have little success. Anyone who hopes to quickly paste together an application or simply speculate about the possibility of fraud is doomed to fail. But if you have a valid case, supported by significant information, and rely on qualified counsel, your odds of success are extremely promising.

Snapshot of the State Reward Program

After a decade of DOJ blazing the trail, many states have modified their programs to help activate the growth of whistleblowers. They are keenly aware that DOJ has recouped over $10 billion under its reward program. Such statistics make this type of a reward program irresistible to the states.

Consequently, a dozen states have recently enacted state fraud reward programs. They are virtually word-for-word the same as the DOJ program. The only significant differences are that the fraud is against the state and the reward is paid in state dollars instead of federal ones.

This is an exciting era for the states, as they are already recovering hundreds of millions of dollars lost due to fraud, thanks to whistleblowers. With the proper research and attention to the process, one of those rewards could come to you.

Snapshot of the IRS Reward Program

This book is one of the first to shed light on the new IRS Reward Program that extends the reach of huge rewards to whistleblowers in the area of unpaid taxes.

You can now partner with the IRS in ways you could not in the past. In the process, you may be eligible to receive a significant monetary reward for reporting underpayments of federal income taxes.

It is believed that as much as $150 billion in taxes are under-reported annually. Citizens like you can receive up to 30 percent of the funds recovered.

Like the primary DOJ Reward Program, the brand new IRS Reward Program has many technical rules and requirements. Although the program is in its infancy, it too is largely modeled after the DOJ program. Thus, an important first step in understanding the IRS Reward Program is to become familiar with the DOJ Reward Program.

You'll find the last section of this book devoted to explaining the eligibility requirements and highlighting the special requirements that differ from the DOJ Reward Program. It also includes checklists and examples to help you become a better partner with the IRS in ensuring others pay their fair share of taxes so that your taxes do not need to be increased to carry their load.

Right for Today

Fifteen years ago, when the DOJ Reward Program was just taking off, I was one of the bright-eyed, young attorneys hired by DOJ in Washington, D.C.

While I was part of that team of competent, highly trained, and dedicated fraud attorneys, I saw the DOJ rewards paid to whistleblowers increased from a meager $10 million to $1.8 billion. It was an exciting time.

While at DOJ, I personally reviewed numerous reward applications in order to make recommendations as to which had merit and how much reward to pay. From the hundreds of cases assigned to me, I investigated allegations of fraud against 20 different federal agencies.

Over the years, I became efficient at quickly distinguishing between cases that were promising and cases we referred to as "dogs." I have gained keen insights into the workings of the DOJ Reward Program that I am sharing with the public for the first time now.

Why Write this Book?

Although it was a great pleasure to work at DOJ, I left with two frustrations.

First, despite the fact that huge awards are paid out every year, the program is still largely unknown to most people.

With hundreds of billions of dollars of undetected fraud, I want to see even more quality applications from those who know about fraud.

Second, many applications fall far short of meeting the requirements or offering any real value. They end up wasting the time of both the government officials and the whistleblower.

I always felt sorry for the individuals who had prepared their case and endured certain risks only to discover they were chasing a mirage — often due to poor preparation and inadequate advice! Because the average time for DOJ to decline a case is two years, these individuals needlessly wasted years of time and energy on false hope.

For over a decade, I have pondered the solutions to these vexing problems. This is my opportunity to share my solutions.

My first objective is to open wide the doors of the DOJ Reward Program by publicly sharing what should not be a secret:

The government wants to partner with you to fight fraud.
If you properly participate, you'll be justly rewarded.

The second objective, which is equally important, is to improve the quality of reward applications by shedding light upon what it takes to meet the requirements of the program. To do so, I will explain why I believe many cases are not attractive to the government. It is my hope that this information will be of help, not only to potential whistleblowers, but to their attorneys and the DOJ attorneys review-ing the cases as well.

Both goals are best realized through a candid discussion of the criteria of the programs, vivid examples of cases the government has embraced, and frank discussions regarding the importance of select-ing counsel. You will find all of those elements in this book.

Are You Eligible?

Before exploring the substance of the reward programs, you may be wondering whether you know something that would make you eligible in one of the programs. In fact, one of the most frequently asked questions is "Am I eligible?" A close second is, "Who knows the type of information that the government needs and is willing to pays rewards?" You might be surprised at the answers. In fact, chances are that you, or someone you know, is in a position to find the type of information needed to make an application to the DOJ, state, or IRS.

Most large companies have government contracts or receive some grants or other government subsidies. You may think, "But my company would never cheat." Maybe not, but the fact remains that nearly every major defense contractor has been sued at least once by the government for fraud. Most major hospitals, even the most respected in the nation, also have been required to repay funds to the government under these programs. The list of frauddoers includes the granddaddy of them all: pharmaceutical companies.

The modern-day reward programs extend to fraud against all 20-some government agencies, plus the myriad of state programs where a reward program has been enacted. Thus, it includes cus-toms fraud, grant fraud (whether education or research), Homeland Security fraud, and fraud against every other agency or government program.

The bottom line is this: the reward programs apply to every company that receives any funds or property from the government. The scope of this book does not end with federal agencies. At least a dozen states have enacted similar reward programs to recapture state funds wrongfully obtained.

Since Congress has now authorized the IRS to revamp its reward program to model it after the DOJ Reward Program, the field has expanded to the ultimate degree. Huge rewards are now available for reporting underpayment of federal taxes. While not everyone knows of a company with government contracts, federal taxes are paid by everyone you know.

You Can Be a Whistleblower

By now, you may be thinking, "I could be a whistleblower…"

You're right. So let me begin by addressing two important questions:

1. Where do you get the information?
2. How can you tell if you have a good case?

Forget about all the movies you have seen. These government reward programs are not action thrillers and modern whistleblowers need not save the world. It makes more sense to imagine a person who is correcting one wrong at a time with the help of others. A whistleblower is not a martyr, but someone who steps forward and truthfully reports when others fail to play by the rules.

Now, put aside everything else you may have read about whistleblowing. Misinformation and misconceptions abound.

There is a good reason why DOJ turns down nearly 80 percent of the applications filed. Most people do not understand these reward programs. They rush to file an application without organizing the information or showing clear evidence of fraud and assume that the government will be able to figure out for itself whether fraud occurred.

This practice cripples the programs and wastes everyone's time. Because the programs are governed by specific laws, it only makes sense that there must be specific rules to follow for fraud to be demonstrated and rewards to be paid.

What you need most is an experienced guide. You need someone who knows how to avoid pitfalls, when a case is worth pursuing, and how to keep people from wasting time and energy. In this book, I will be your guide. I will draw from my 15-year service within the DOJ office administering the federal reward program at its headquarters in Washington, D.C.

A Team Approach

A modern-day whistleblower does not need to uncover the entire plot and neatly wrap up all lose ends with fancy ribbons to place a

Christmas present under the tree for a prosecuting attorney. The whistleblower proves his worth by teaming up with the government. They are the ones taking the initiative by reporting that fraud is afoot. By providing some concrete information, they end up jumpstarting a government investigation.

The place where many gather facts giving rise to fraud is when they are asked to do something by a supervisor that raises a red flag. In other words, they are asked to carry out orders that they know are wrong and result in the government paying out money it should not have to. Others come across the information during discussions with co-workers who were asked to do something wrong. Regardless of what sets off the bells in your head, often just a little additional probing is often all that is needed to perfect your readiness to step forward.

In one of the first cases I worked on at DOJ, a whistleblower brought little more than a piece of paper to the government's attention. It was an internal document summarizing costs for one of its large government projects. What caught the whistleblower's eye was the line item named "reserve." The whistleblower didn't know a lot about what it meant, only that it would be improper to pad estimates with an undisclosed reserve when negotiating a sole-source government contract.

After presenting this document to DOJ, the whistleblower basically sat back and allowed the DOJ attorneys to do what they were hired to do — combat fraud.

I was one of those government attorneys assembling a team of investigators and auditors. Together, we served subpoenas, reviewed many boxes of documents, interviewed witnesses, and took depositions. Several years later, the company paid back more than $50 million. The whistleblower received over $7 million as a DOJ reward.

Ready to Begin?

Are you ready to take the next step?

Would you like to find out if you have what you need to be eligible for a reward?

If you take the time necessary to read this book carefully, you will be able to understand for yourself the nature and requirements of these reward programs.

It is important to read it in order, because all of the reward programs are modeled after the DOJ program and the chapters build one upon another. By the last chapter, you will be ready to assess whether you have the information the government is willing to pay large rewards.

SECTION ONE:
The Federal Reward Program

CHAPTER TWO

Case Study:
The DOJ Reward Program

Where there are laws, he who has not broken them need not tremble.

— VITTORIO ALFIER

Want to know more about a government program with rewards so large you could retire?

Let me give you an example. The story that follows illustrates the interplay between a modern-day whistleblower and the DOJ attorneys. It clearly demonstrates what it takes to receive a significant reward under government reward programs. In the chapters that follow, I will articulate the steps you need to improve your chances of receiving the astonishing rewards that are possible in this little-known, but powerful, DOJ Reward Program.

The Hidden Reserve
First Contact

Dressed in brown polyester pants and a worn sports coat, Mr. Jamison paused before passing through the marble columns at the entrance of the Department of Justice in Washington D.C. His attorney, John Duncan, held the door open and smiled. "Everything will be all right. I'll be with you every step of the way."

It was reassuring, but Mr. Jamison's heart still fluttered as he walked past the rows and rows of photographs of former U.S. Presidents and United States Attorneys that hung in the hallways. The towering ceilings seemed to reach to the heavens. Even the corridors were wider than most rooms in Mr. Jamison's home. The magnitude of the buildings and the power of the government seemed to press upon his shoulders. It was an impression that would remain with him forever.

When Mr. Jamison entered an equally impressive conference room, he could not help but notice the prominent flags of the United States and the Department of Justice. Seated behind polished wood tables were two neatly dressed men who stood when he and Mr. Duncan walked in.

FBI Special Agent Rusk came forward and firmly gripped Mr. Jamison's hand. A young man dressed in a crisp blue suit introduced himself as well. "Hello. My name is Mr. Hanson, trial attorney for the Department of Justice."

In a deep voice, Agent Rusk began the conversation. "We've read your attorney's legal filings and application for a reward. We understand you allege fraud by FlyX, one of the leading defense firms in the city. Can you explain the fraud to us?"

Now that the moment had arrived, Mr. Jamison felt a little intimidated. It was hard to believe that, just weeks after talking to his lawyer about possible fraud, he was actually seated with an FBI agent and a DOJ attorney. It seemed so surreal.

His attorney, Mr. Duncan, spoke for him. "Yes, we are here to provide you with information we believe you will find helpful to recover millions of dollars that FlyX overcharged the Department of Defense on flight simulators."

Mr. Duncan was poised to continue, but the DOJ attorney interrupted. "Thank you, Mr. Duncan. But if you don't mind, I would like to hear from Mr. Jamison." He leaned forward. Looking Mr. Jamison straight in his eyes, he asked, "Explain in your own words. What did FlyX do that you think was wrong?"

Mr. Jamison explained that the company had cheated in bidding on several contracts to build flight simulators to train military pilots.

As he was struggling for just the right way to explain the fraud, his attorney suggested, "Why don't you show them the documents you have?"

The Smoking Gun

A hint of a smile came over the face of the government attorney. DOJ Attorney Hanson knew the importance of documents to prove a case. He was hoping for a real smoking gun, but would be pleased with any head start on a fraud investigation.

Mr. Jamison pulled out a single piece of paper. It was entitled "Bid Summary Sheet." It had two columns. One column had the heading "Financial Program Plan" and the other column read "Contract Value." There were many descriptive line items on the page, broken down by labor and material. Under the first column, the total labor costs were $7 million. But the Contract Value figure was $7.7 million. For the material costs, both columns were the same amount.

The DOJ Attorney Hanson asked Mr. Jamison to explain the two columns. Mr. Jamison smiled broadly as he stated, "The Financial Program Plan is the company's real best estimate of labor costs to build the flight simulators. The Contract Value is the estimated cost FlyX told the government."

Mr. Hanson interrupted. "I am not sure I am following you. Can you state it another way?"

"Sure," Mr. Jamison said, warming to his topic. Soon he was on a roll. Mr. Jamison explained that the contract is a sole-source bid and no one really knew how much it would cost to build something that had not been built before. So, the military had asked FlyX to come up with its best estimate of the costs and to detail how it arrived at them. Based on that, the military would negotiate a fair contract price.

DOJ Attorney Hanson interrupted again. "And what do these two columns mean?"

Mr. Jamison pointed to the first one. "The Financial Program Plan is what FlyX estimated — mind you, after months of study and calculations. It is what the company actually estimated for the labor costs." Moving his finger to the next column, Mr. Jamison added, "But this one, the Contract Value column, is what it *told the government* its labor cost estimate was."

The eyes of Agent Rusk widened. He leaned forward. "Can you prove that?"

Mr. Jamison was taken aback a bit. "Well, it says so right here."

Mr. Duncan motioned for Mr. Jamison to stop. "Why don't you explain the bottom part of the document?"

Mr. Jamison exclaimed, "Oh, yeah. At the bottom of the document there is a line labeled 'risk/reserve.' This amount just happens to be the difference between the totals of the Financial Program Plan column and the Contract Value column." Mr. Jamison added, "Don't you see? The $700,000 amount listed under reserve is how much FlyX padded its estimated labor costs!"

DOJ Attorney Hanson's brows puckered slightly, examining the document. This was starting to look like something after all. He asked Mr. Jamison to explain what the term risk/reserve meant.

Mr. Jamison explained it was the negotiation reserve. He said that this practice had started years ago, when a new contracting officer had taken over. The contracting officer had bragged that he could knock off ten percent from any cost estimate during contract negotiations. He was out to make a name for himself in an effort to make Colonel one day. "I heard that upper management was scared. They felt it unfair to require the company to spend five months making up an estimate in good faith only to have the contracting officer subtract an automatic ten percent." Even after the contracting officer left, the practice continued. "The way I see it, FlyX padded all of its labor cost estimates by ten percent to be able to give something up to the contracting officer and make him feel good about the contract price."

DOJ Attorney Hanson rubbed his chin, still staring intently at the document. After a few moments of deep reflection, he asked, "What other proof do you have?"

Mr. Jamison spoke for several minutes about meetings he attended where it was discussed that after true estimates were prepared the negotiation team would inflate them.

His lawyer added more details about the fraud scheme. Afterwards, Mr. Duncan summarized, "You can prove this pretty easily. After all, the company spent months coming up with its real estimates. All you need to do is subpoena the files and compare the numbers. If they match the Financial Plan numbers, you've got them." He paused for a moment, then added, "And it's not limited to this one contract. We think they added a negotiation reserve on *all* of their sole-source contracts. That means they cheated by some $100 million."

Mr. Duncan outlined for the government an investigative strategy and then handed the FBI agent a folder detailing the fraud allegations and containing copies of documents supporting the case.

What Next?

The meeting ended quickly and the DOJ attorney told Mr. Jamison's attorney that he would be in touch.

After they left the building, Mr. Jamison asked Mr. Duncan how he felt things went. "It's in their hands now," Mr. Duncan said. "We did all we could. Besides, how can they resist that smoking gun document?"

A few doubts lingered in Mr. Jamison's mind. He feared that the government would not take the case and that the taxpayers had paid too much for the contract. He also wondered what would happen to him. As part of the reward process, he had had to list his name in the suit filed by his attorney claiming the overpayments. It would just be a matter of time before the world knew that he had blown the whistle.

Mr. Duncan assured his client that he did the right thing. He also reassured Mr. Jamison that he would be in his corner at every step. Mr. Jamison vowed to ensure that the government would receive his full support and that he would work closely with the FBI agent. Mr. Jamison felt relieved. He was not alone.

First Impressions

In the meantime, the mood at DOJ was emphatically upbeat. Immediately after the meeting with Mr. Jamison, the DOJ attorney asked Agent Rusk what he thought of the allegations.

"Well, it isn't everyday you get a smoking gun handed to you on a platter!" Rusk said. "But what about the source? What do you think of Mr. Jamison?"

The DOJ attorney smiled. "He's a work of art. A bit like Columbo in terms of style and way of speaking. I'd never put him on the stand. But, I never count on that in these types of cases anyway. If the document checks out, FlyX will be writing one big check!" The FBI agent also commented upon the quality of Mr. Duncan. "He really did his homework." The DOJ attorney added, "I think he will be a valuable asset."

An Open Case

The agent and DOJ attorney spent the next few weeks mapping out an investigative plan. They would need several auditors, a few more investigators and maybe even the help of another DOJ attorney or two. Then they would need to draft subpoenas and get the agency on board.

During the next few weeks, the DOJ attorney made several calls to Mr. Duncan for more information and to discuss strategy. Mr. Duncan performed many other tasks, such as preparing an outline for the government regarding what documents to subpoena.

After assembling a strike force, it was time to move into action. Half-a-dozen agents arrived simultaneously at the homes of six FlyX employees. They were people Mr. Jamison had named as potentially having relevant knowledge and a willingness to tell the truth. The government needed to get to them fast before the company "lawyered up."

Typically, when a company gets wind of a federal investigation, they hold a meeting with the employees, conditioning them to the company's position and telling them not to talk to the government without a corporate attorney present. Usually employees clam up at this point, fearing for their jobs if they talk to the government.

The sweep paid off. Two people admitted that they had known there was a negotiation reserve and that the true estimates might be different from the ones given to the military. The government had corroboration.

Striking Gold

A few months later, an FBI agent served a subpoena on the company. It sought the estimated labor costs for all of its contracts over the last ten years. It also asked for copies of any memos regarding negotiation reserves or difference between Financial Program Plan and Contract Values.

It took several months for FlyX to produce the requested documents. Initially, it provided DOJ with 40 boxes of papers regarding dozens of contracts. It seemed like a lot, even for a $100 million dollar case spanning dozens of contracts. The production was viewed by the government as stonewalling — an attempt by FlyX to "bury the government in paper," so they wouldn't be able to find what they were looking for. It was a stalling tactic. The DOJ attorney asked Mr. Duncan to help review the 40 boxes of documents. Mr. Duncan was able to point out the significance of many documents. He also informed the government that FlyX failed to produce any of the summary sheets Mr. Jamison gave to the government.

DOJ contacted the company and complained that the production was deficient and threatened to ask a judge to compel full production. Three weeks later, two more boxes trickled in, followed by a steady stream of more.

In some of the later boxes, the government finally found summary sheets for several of the contracts. Other relevant internal memos and missing links began showing up as well. Although it would take two auditors several months of full-time work, eventually, they were able to piece together the true estimated labor costs. They matched them up with the Financial Program Plan columns.

Business-Decision Time

FlyX could not escape the conclusion that it had failed to report its true best estimates in violation of the Truth in Negotiation Act. However, it refused to repay any funds. It took the position that, since the ultimate contract price was at or below its real estimates, there had been no harm to the government — even if there had been a technical violation of the law. FlyX had clearly made the decision that it would be cheaper to litigate, at least for now, than to settle. Lawyers for FlyX liked their chances of convincing a court that there was no actual loss to the government.

The Long Haul

Mr. Duncan volunteered to research FlyX's defenses. He helped DOJ determine that the fraud claims were on solid ground. DOJ was not dissuaded by FlyX digging in its heals, nor was it intimidated by the large law firms hired to defend the company. Instead, DOJ intervened and took over Mr. Jamison's lawsuit against FlyX, then went about the business of aggressive litigation.

After DOJ formally served the civil complaint, FlyX began its counterattack. It filed numerous motions to dismiss the suit. FlyX was intent on proving that, because there had been no damage, there could be no case.

It also set its sights upon Mr. Jamison. It didn't want him to receive a dime for helping DOJ. It took his deposition, then filed a motion to disqualify Mr. Jamison from receiving a reward under the statute. FlyX argued that Mr. Jamison did not have direct and independent knowledge of the alleged fraud, which it argued was a requirement in every reward application. It claimed that Mr. Jamison was not eligible for a DOJ reward as a matter of law.

The litigation became fierce. DOJ assigned three more attorneys to the case, as the pace of depositions increased to the point that more than one deposition was going on simultaneously. Both sides waited eagerly for the judge's rulings.

The Defining Moment

After a year of active litigation, the judge issued rulings denying FlyX's motions to dismiss. The first ruling was a giant victory for the government.

The court held that the military had been damaged by the lies and hidden reserves of FlyX. It didn't matter that negotiations had ended up below the company's true best estimates. In fact, the court said that there was a presumption that the government would have negotiated a dollar-for-dollar reduction in price regardless of the starting point. Therefore, the loss would be the amount of the negotiation reserve for each contract. That could be $70 million or more for the contracts in question.

This was great news for DOJ. But would Mr. Jamison be entitled to a reward? The court issued a separate order denying FlyX's motion to dismiss Mr. Jamison. The judge ruled that Mr. Jamison was eligible under the DOJ Reward Program. It was not necessary for Mr. Jamison to prove that he had direct and independent knowledge because he had come forward before the allegations were publicly disclosed. Therefore, the court did not need to decide whether or not his production of the summary sheet was sufficient knowledge to meet the original source rule. This meant that Mr. Jamison was guaranteed a slice of the pie. He would get between 15 and 25 percent of whatever DOJ collected back from FlyX.

Under the False Claims Act FlyX would have to pay *triple the amount of loss*. Therefore, the company was facing liability in the neighborhood of $210 million.

The Final Chapter

About this time, FlyX filed for bankruptcy. It is hard to determine whether this was part of a strategy of reducing the amount it may pay in a settlement to DOJ or if the huge expenses from hiring outside law firms had weighed too heavily upon the company. But one thing was certain. FlyX would not be able to afford to pay the full amount of a judgment.

Based upon the new court rulings, FlyX needed to make a series of new business decisions relating to the lawsuit. FlyX told DOJ that it was time to settle.

DOJ knew that it would have to take less than what it might have won at trial. For one thing, bankruptcy rules would limit the amount DOJ could recover, but the DOJ also had a policy of not intentionally shutting down legitimate companies. The question was, what amount could FlyX afford to pay and still keep its doors open? After several weeks of negotiations, the parties arrived at a settlement of $70 million.

As soon as it received the money, the DOJ attorney was pleased to wire the reward to Mr. Jamison's attorney. As a whistleblower, it was his rightful share of the money the government had recovered.

Without Mr. Jamison, the government would not have known about and proven the fraud and would not have received the $70 million settlement. Paying Mr. Jamison made sense. It was a good return on the government's investment. Mr. Jamison's reward for being a whistleblower was $13 million.

News that a modern day-whistleblower had become a multi-millionaire was good press. Perhaps other companies will think twice. Perhaps other potential whistleblowers might be willing to step forward to report other fraud.

As a result of the case, FlyX also changed its bidding practices and continued providing the military with much-needed quality flight simulators. It was a win-win situation for everyone.

CHAPTER THREE

Overview: Obtaining a DOJ Reward

An idealist is a person who helps other people to be prosperous.

— HENRY FORD (1863–1947)

A few years ago, a medical worker named John walked into his lawyer's office with an internal corporate document proving the hospital's deliberate participation in fraud. The memo directed the coding clerk at the hospital to add a bogus blood test to every Medicare patient's billing record. Knowing that this kind of practice was unethical and illegal, John kept a copy of the document and, through his attorney, reported it to the authorities.

Three years later, the DOJ awarded John with $5 million.

Although this scene doesn't happen every day, it occurs frequently enough that the DOJ has paid a total of $1.8 billion in rewards. Every year the Department of Justice pays out hundreds of millions of dollars in rewards. And there is no sign that these mega-awards will be ending any time soon.

According to raw statistics, one out of five people who file an application under the DOJ Reward Program receive a reward. Of those receiving rewards, one out of five make over a million dollars. In fact, the overall average — when all the rewards are divided by the number of people receiving a reward — is $1.75 million.

This means that about 1 in 25 people who apply for a DOJ reward become millionaires.

While 1 in 25 is far better odds than playing the lottery or *Texas Hold'em* poker tournaments, "winning" is not simple.

You have to know what to look for. Not every type of unethical practice or fraud is eligible for a reward. When you do apply, you must follow the steps very carefully. Four out of five people who apply for an award fail to receive it because of errors on their application or they don't have the right type of case.

Sometimes, the DOJ program can seem like a maze without guide posts. That's why this book was written. It not only identifies the rules, but provides a detailed game plan for reaching the reward at the end.

Fulfilling a Unique Role

This book was created to help whistleblowers like you navigate the process successfully and receive your reward. As a 15-year veteran attorney of the DOJ office in Washington, D.C., administering this nationwide reward program, I will be your guide.

I will explain the type of information you need and the manner in which you must present it to be eligible for a DOJ reward. I also explore with you the risks that must be balanced against the potential rewards to help you decide whether it is worth the effort to apply. I will map out the path you must follow, should you decide to step forward. I will also use plenty of illustrations to ensure you understand the points being made.

In the few hours it takes to read this book, you'll become familiar with this remarkable reward statute and find the answers to your questions. In the end, you will be poised to take the next step of contacting an experienced attorney to evaluate your particular case and help you make an informed decision.

It is my personal hope that you will also come away with a better appreciation for the types of fraud that harm our government programs. Always keep in mind, that when you receive a DOJ reward, it is because you have joined with DOJ in the fight against fraud.

In a Nutshell

Why does DOJ pay such huge rewards? The short answer is that the government is losing such an enormous amount of money because of fraud that it can pay generous rewards and still come out ahead.

It is estimated that as much as ten percent of Medicare bills contain fraudulent amounts. That translates into tens of billions of tax dollars lost each year. And fraud is not limited to just Medicare. Every government agency — including the military, the Department of Energy, and even the post office — has its share of companies committing fraud.

Congress recognized that the public was in the best position to help the government prove fraud. It voted to reward the very people these cheating companies were forcing to commit fraud. Thus, a whistleblower reward statute was born. Actually, the law was first introduced by Abraham Lincoln in 1863. It wasn't until recently that the False Claims Act statute was modernized to open up opportunities for average citizens to participate. In 1986, it was rewritten to meet the needs of modern-day whistleblowers. Since then, people from all walks of life are receiving large rewards for doing the right thing.

The benefit of using the carrot of a reward to combat fraud has proven remarkably successful. By paying over $1.8 billion in rewards, DOJ has reclaimed more than $11 billion dollars in fraudulently obtained funds. In one year, DOJ paid out $325 million in whistleblower rewards to recoup close to $2 billion in payments obtained by false pretenses. The program is working so effectively that state governments and the IRS have adopted similar citizen reward programs.

Inexperience Hurts

Reporting fraud under this DOJ Reward Program is not as simple as picking up the telephone and calling a hotline. You must select a qualified whistleblower attorney to organize your allegations and prepare complex legal filings. Your attorney must then convincingly present your case to an assigned DOJ attorney and continue to help prove the fraud and recover the ill-gotten gains.

Sadly, most whistleblowers are ill prepared for the task. They simply fail to understand DOJ's perspective, practices, and policies. Some inexperienced attorneys mean well, but rush the process and end up creating a mediocre application receiving little attention. A few attorneys misunderstand the process and incorrectly view it as a game of outwitting DOJ. They thwart the process by failing to become team players. Still others are so myopically focused upon the technical aspects that they lose sight of the spirit of the program. As a result, four out of five applications are rejected by DOJ.

Balancing Risks and Rewards

The axiom "All that glitters is not gold" is true. Reporting fraud is a big decision. Not every case is successful. There are many factors to consider. To guide you in this process, I will take you through the personal issues which matter most to you by addressing issues of attorney fees and taxes, as well as the risks a whistleblower might encounter. This will help you judge if it's worth your effort. You'll also learn ways to minimize risks. Often, just knowing what lies ahead dispels fear. Having a proper attitude and patience will go a long way in making the process of joining the growing ranks of modern-day whistleblowers more pleasant.

There is much to cover, so let's begin finding out whether you should apply for a DOJ reward and how to do it.

CHAPTER FOUR
A Quick Peek at Real Sample Cases

Money dishonestly acquired is never worth its cost, while a good conscience never costs as much as it is worth.

— JEAN PETIT SENN

In 1990, when I joined the Civil Fraud Section, DOJ had paid out a total of just under $10 million dollars in rewards. Those rewards, however, resulted in $40 million in additional recoveries from wrong-doers. It was not a bad return on the investment, and it proved to be just the tip of the iceberg.

By the time I left DOJ, the rewards paid to citizens had swelled to $1.8 billion. DOJ is now recovering over a billion dollars a year from wrongdoers and paying rewards of $250 million a year. From just a sampling of the cases I worked on, the people who did step forward received these remarkable rewards:

> **$100 Million.** Two whistleblowers told DOJ that a large hospital chain was including unallowable costs in its annual Medicare cost reports. The hospitals were keeping two sets of books, one submitted to the government and another set containing the true costs.

> **$67 Million.** Several whistleblowers reported that a dozen major oil companies were underpaying the royalties owed to the Department of Interior for drilling oil on federal land.

$7.5 Million. While working for a major pharmaceutical company, a whistleblower learned that the company was not reporting to Medicaid its true "best price" for each of its drugs. Drug companies are supposed to give Medicaid the same price as they give their best customers. This company tried concealing its true price on one sale by offering a so-called "educational grant" to the hospital to make the price of the drugs appear higher. In the end, it did not report the true price of the drug sold to a hospital. DOJ opened an investigation and learned that the fraud was more extensive than it first appeared. The pharmaceutical company was overcharging Medicaid tens of millions of dollars.

$1.5 Million. After a whistleblower reported that his company was not properly testing parts to be used by the military, as required by the contract, DOJ recovered $7 million from the company.

$1 Million. In two different grant fraud cases against a top university and a highly respected teaching hospital, whistle-blowers were given $1 million each for identifying ways these entities used federal grant money for purposes outside the scope of the grants.

$830,000. A company hired to repair military aircraft realized it could not account for all of the government engine parts in its shop, so it made the bad decision to alter its inventory records to try and conceal the lost parts. Under the contract, the company was liable for lost or stolen parts. By altering the records and lying about which parts it had received, the company did not disclose and pay for missing parts.

$500,000. Two additional Medicare fraud matters are of interest. In the first case, several doctors were billing Medicare for services they did not actually provide. In the second case, a hospital was routinely billing observation charges to all of its outpatient procedures regardless of whether there was a medical need.

As you can see, DOJ pays big rewards for reporting fraud against government programs of every type in the hopes of collecting back misused federal funds. Clearly, the DOJ Reward Program has been hugely successful and should continue for the foreseeable future. The only limitation is whether modern-day whistleblowers will keep stepping forward.

CHAPTER FIVE

Origin of the DOJ Reward Program

Law cannot persuade where it cannot punish.

— THOMAS FULLER

The chief tool of the federal government for combating fraud is the False Claims Act. Because fraud claims are often brought to the government's attention by whistleblowers, this act is often referred to as the *DOJ Reward Program*. To encourage people to report fraud, in an average case which DOJ takes the lead, the DOJ Reward Program permits DOJ to pay rewards between 15 and 25 percent of the entire amount of funds it recovers.

The False Claims Act provides that anyone who knowingly submits a false claim to the federal government is liable to repay *three times the amount of the loss* suffered by the government. It also allows DOJ to collect civil penalties of up to $11,000 for each false claim submitted by the wrongdoer. With penalties like these, it is easy to see why this law, with its sharp teeth, is a favorite of DOJ.

The False Claims Act is designed to deter companies from cheating the government and hit them hard in the pocketbook if they fail to heed the warnings.

Suppose an aerospace company is hired to repair military fighter jets. It submits invoices twice a month for a year. Because it has underbid the project and doesn't want to lose money, it decides to add to its invoices labor charges for ten employees who were actually working on other projects. If the employees' salaries were $50,000 each, the charges would inflate the invoice by $500,000. If the fraud is revealed, the government will be able to recover three times the falsely charged costs, plus penalties.

The company could be required to pay three times $500,000, for a total of $1.5 million ($50,000 x 10 x 3). The company would also be subject to up to $11,000 for each false claim. In this case, each invoice is a false claim. So the total penalties would be $264,000 (24 invoices x $11,000).

This means that the company could be forced to repay $1.75 million in a case where the actual fraud amounted to $500,000. If the fraud occurred for ten years, the amount of repayment could be ten times this amount.

If the government recovered this money, the whistleblower who observed and reported this fraud could be eligible for between 15 and 25 percent of the entire amount. In this case, the reward could be approximately $260,000 to $435,000.

The Early History

During the Civil War the government had been billed for worthless (and sometimes nonexistent) goods. Abraham Lincoln was outraged to realize that some citizens would stoop to robbing the government in a time of war. Out of a desire to punish the offenders, they established a law which allowed the government to recover *double* the amount of the fraud.

While this amount was less than in today's law, its reward for reporting the fraud was greater. It gave early whistleblowers 50 percent of the recovered monies. The law contained a landmark provision permitting private citizens to file suit on behalf of the government and then split the proceeds evenly.

The action filed by the citizen was called a *qui tam*, from a Latin phrase meaning: "He who pursues a matter on behalf of the King, as well as for himself." (The most common pronunciation of *qui tam* is "kwee tom," but it is often pronounced "key tam" or "kwee tam.")

Then, as now, the rationale for the DOJ Reward Program was the notion that the best way to catch a thief was to reward an associate. In other words, it was "sending a rogue to catch a rogue."

Unfortunately, this early law did not allow DOJ to help the whistle-blower prosecute the case. Rather, the whistleblower had to fund, prosecute, and prove the entire fraud case to obtain a reward. This proved too high a hurdle. Without the legal resources and expertise of the DOJ, very few citizens had the wherewithal to proceed. So the program languished for a century.

In 1986, Senator Charles E. Grassley (R. Iowa) and Congressman Howard Berman (D. CA) championed the cause by combating rampant fraud among government contractors. Their efforts caused the reward program to be reborn, and it became much easier for average citizens to step forward and report fraud. Because the DOJ now shoulders the burden of investigation and prosecution, modern-day whistleblowers are under far less pressure.

Changes were also made to greatly increase the availability of rewards, creating three ranges of rewards, including up to 30 percent when the whistleblower handles the case, 25 percent in instances where DOJ primarily handles the case, and ten percent when the whistleblower brings very little to the table. As a further enticement, the new law has added a section prohibiting an employer from retaliating against a whistleblower. It carries stiff penalties for any violations. In addition, because DOJ is now a partner, employers often think better of trying to retaliate.

In sum, DOJ now broadcasts a clear "whistleblowers are welcome" signal, inviting whistleblowers to step forward and collect sizeable rewards for reporting fraud.

Almost as soon as the ink was dry on the newly amended law, many *qui tams* were filed. Within the first year, there were 32 *qui tam* suits. The number doubled the next year. The ranks of whistleblowers kept swelling and the amount of rewards kept skyrocketing to the present day where DOJ is paying hundreds of millions a year in rewards to average citizens, just like you.

The DOJ Reward Program does not have a cap or ceiling. It will pay as much in rewards as there are good fraud cases being reported. In simple terms, the amount of the reward you may hope to receive will depend solely upon the quality of your individual application. Because there is between $10 and $100 billion a year being lost to fraud, the DOJ could afford to pay much more in rewards. That means there are plenty of opportunities for you to link up with DOJ and help protect government programs and taxpayer's funds.

Honest Abe's Right Idea is Right for Today

Abraham Lincoln had the right idea, but the statute was wrongly worded. If Lincoln had allowed citizens to report fraud and allowed DOJ attorneys to link together with them, the law would have worked as effectively in the 19th century as it does today. Now, the DOJ Reward Program is so effective that 60 percent of all fraudulent payments recovered by DOJ are the result of whistleblowers stepping forward and reporting fraud.

The revised reward program makes things much easier for you, as a whistleblower. It is important, however, that you meticulously follow the procedures. Again, eight out of ten applicants have failed to meet the requirements. But for those who properly evaluate and bring a case meeting the *Four F Factors*, the rewards can be very exciting. The next chapters will walk you through the process.

CHAPTER SIX
The *"Four F Factors"* of Eligibility

Never spend your money before you have it.

— THOMAS JEFFERSON

Although the general concept of paying rewards for reporting fraud is simple, the DOJ Reward Program is not intuitive. It is actually quite complex, especially when it is applied to real-life situations. Navigating the program requires significant special skill, knowledge and experience.

Without attempting to describe all of the nuances, I'll describe some of the DOJ policies and practices that are worth highlighting, so you gain proper insight into the program.

The Four F Factors

If we distill the DOJ Reward Program down into its core components, there are four factors necessary for a whistleblower to gain the attention of DOJ and receive a reward. I call these key elements the *Four F Factors*:

Filing first
Format is fundamentally correct
Fraud under a federal program
Funds are forfeited

If a single one of these *F Factors* is missing, your case will fail. That doesn't mean, of course, that having all *Four F Factors* will guarantee you a reward.

The *Four F Factors* will simply have the greatest impact upon whether DOJ looks favorably upon your case. Knowing how to enhance these factors should greatly help you develop a winning submission.

Filing First

Congress has decided that only one whistleblower is eligible to receive a reward for each particular instance of fraud. To avoid subjectively deciding which person provided the most helpful information, the reward statute favors paying the first person to file an action *(qui tam)*.

It is this simple: If someone else already filed a *qui tam* on the same fraud allegation, you won't be eligible for a reward. By the same token, if you file a proper complaint first, you won't have to share your reward with anyone else.

In some instances, the *First to File Rule* has resulted in a race to the courthouse. However, you must guard against the temptation of rushing the application process. This first *F Factor* is only one of several barriers to becoming a successful whistleblower. It will do you little good to be the first to file an action, only to be rejected a year later when flaws surface. Never forget, DOJ declines over 75 percent of the first applications filed because they are filled with flaws.

Racing too hard to beat a hypothetical whistleblower can actually thwart your overall chance of receiving a reward. Still, you should not delay in contacting qualified counsel to begin the process of preparing a timely and quality application.

Actually, your best defense in the first to file setting is not to speed up the process, but to slow down your mouth!

Let me explain. As a whistleblower starts contemplating the possibility of filing a *qui tam*, they tend to start talking about it. They may even tell another person the whole fraudulent scheme in vivid detail. Gossip travels fast and loose lips sink ships. With potentially enormous rewards at stake, what is to prevent someone else from contacting a lawyer using your information?

I would venture to guess that more races to the courthouse are lost through a whistleblower's own loose lips than because of someone else having the same prior notion of the fraud. More often than not, several people know about a given fraud. What they don't know about is the DOJ Reward Program.

Ted was an example of this. One day, while he was reading the newspaper over breakfast, he saw that an employee at the hospital where Ted worked had filed a *qui tam* suit, alleging that the hospital was improperly adding an X-ray charge to every Medicare bill.

Ted slapped his hand on his knee. "I knew about this! In fact, I knew a lot more about it than he did. I should've reported it!" He winced to see that the reward was likely to be over $300,000.

But all is not lost for Ted. It's true that he could not file a claim at this point — even if he adds more details about the fraud. He would be barred by the first to file rule. However, Ted could still file a *qui tam* alleging other fraud by the same hospital. The odds are, that if a large organization like a hospital is committing systematic fraud in one area, there may be other fraudulent practices going on. Perhaps the hospital is paying kickbacks for referrals or adding fraudulent blood tests to Medicare patients' bills. With a little investigation, Ted may well uncover other fraudulent practices that would represent significant claims.

Format is Fundamentally Correct

Keep in mind that *qui tam* provisions are very exacting. A single misstep can render you ineligible. Many people incorrectly think that they simply need to call an agency hotline to be eligible for a reward. However, to qualify for the huge rewards available under DOJ's program, your attorney must actually bring a civil lawsuit on behalf of the government alleging in detail that someone violated the False Claims Act. This is not something that can be done overnight.

There are two other important things to do besides filing a *qui tam* complaint. Your attorney should notify the government in advance that you have allegations of fraud against a person or company. You also must provide the government with a "written disclosure of substantially all material evidence and information" in your possession relating to the allegations.

More than one whistleblower has been kicked out for failing to scrupulously follow these procedures. They are in fact more than mere technical requirements. They serve the purpose of inviting DOJ to team up with you. Remember, the ultimate goal is to enlist DOJ to take the case and use its resources to recover the funds wrongfully obtained by the defendant.

Hundreds of applications are filed each year and only those that shine make it to the top of DOJ's pile. It is important to find an attorney who will help you evaluate the viability of your case, as much as possible, before going further. They must then work cooperatively with DOJ.

Often out of inexperience, many fail to present persuasive evidence in their applications. I cannot overstate the importance that the application must be compelling to persuade the DOJ attorney to champion the case.

For example, suppose Jill hires an attorney to file a lawsuit for fraud in district court on behalf of the United States. If all of her "evidence" is based on a rumor that her company might be double billing for products on a military contract, her application will be too vague to support the allegations.

If however, Jill's attorney points out that she needs proof and guides her to gather specific facts, she may be eligible for a DOJ reward. The key is that the claim must allege the fraud in sufficient detail to show that the defendant cheated. You should be prepared to show the what, when, why, where, and how of the fraud if you want to support a valid claim.

Do not fall prey to relying upon an inexperienced attorney who files a poorly prepared application. There is no guarantee that your application will be rewarded, regardless of your attorney's efforts. But be sure to find an attorney who has significant experience with the DOJ Reward Program, someone who will actively help you determine whether you meet these criteria and direct you in gathering additional support prior to filing if you don't.

Fraud under a Federal Program

The third *F Factor* is that the whistleblower must allege (and the DOJ ultimately prove) that actionable fraud occurred under a federal contract or program. There are two important elements here.

1. You must go beyond mere suspicion and actually show that the claims were false.

2. You must establish that the federal government was harmed by the fraud in a manner that can be quantified monetarily.

The federal False Claims Act only applies to fraud against the federal government. It does not extend to fraud against companies or individuals. For instance, it does not apply to Internet fraud where people are tricked into giving out bank information. It does not apply to securities fraud, as in the Enron case, where corporate executives cheated stockholders. Similarly, the DOJ program would not apply to the situation in the movie *Erin Brockovich*, where the fraud was against citizens of a community. The key is that there must be federal funds that were falsely obtained or retained.

Take, for example, the fictitious example of EZ-1.com, a large stock trading company. It encourages its customers to buy shares of stock in a new company. What it doesn't say, however, is that it owns shares of the company and that its financial statements are inflated. Millions buy the stock. Within months, the company goes out of business. The company did not fold before EZ-1.com unloaded its shares, but EZ-1.com was aware that the statements were inflated and it did not declare its vested interest to its customers, when it encouraged them to buy stock in the company.

While this would violate the security rules and amount to a form of fraud, it would not be actionable under the False Claims Act and DOJ Reward Program. The funds at issue do not belong to the federal government.

If, however, EZ-1.com were to improperly inflate the price of securities above fair market value (a practice known as "yield burning") and any agency of the government were to pay that price under a federal program, then federal funds would be involved and the case would fall within the False Claims Act. A whistleblower would be entitled to a share of the amount of federal funds recovered by DOJ.

Fraud is Not Isolated

There are many places to be on the lookout for fraud involving federal funds. More than 20 federal agencies spend federal funds. The False Claims Act applies to each one of them. For instance, many companies receive funds from the military or Medicare, and every company uses the post office. If there is cheating on any one of these programs, you could receive a reward for reporting fraud.

Wrongfully Paid Funds

For a DOJ reward to be paid there must be federal funds that were "wrongfully" paid to a company. Of course, companies are equally liable for making statements to retain funds or property that they are not entitled to keep. This is referred to as a "reverse false claim." For example, companies are sometimes required to account for government furnished items. They are liable if they conceal shortages. If they lie to keep from repaying funds for lost or stolen government property, they are liable under the whistle-blower law.

The reach of the program is so broad that the False Claims Act even extends to situations where the government mistakenly sends checks under government programs and the recipient cashes and keeps the funds.

Under the False Claims Act, triple damages are assessed when a person or company is found to have knowingly submitted false claims. The key to proving fraud under the DOJ program requires proof that a defendant knowingly presented a false claim for payment to the federal government. Although the False Claims Act lists seven ways such a violation can occur, the essence is that a person must know that they are not entitled to receive or retain the federal funds or property.

If, for example, a company submits a progress payment report stating that a government contract is 80 percent complete, when it knows the contract is not even halfway done, it has knowingly submitted a false statement in order to immediately receive 80 percent of the contract value. If you can show that the company lied to get paid early, you are likely to have a good case. The only remaining issue in this instance is whether the amount of harm is large enough to warrant DOJ's time.

Deliberate Ignorance

While the False Claims Act is a fraud-based statute, the government does not need to prove that the defendant actually knew it was committing fraud. A violation occurs if the person or company acts with "deliberate ignorance" or "in reckless disregard" of the truth of falsity of the information. In other words, a person is liable if they simply buried their head in the sand to avoid actually knowing that the claim was false. This is a lesser burden of proof than showing that a company intended to cheat.

Although the legal standard to win a *qui tam* case is less than the common definition of fraud, for purposes of this book it remains useful to use the term "fraud" when discussing the reward statutes. The distinction between fraud and "deliberate ignorance" or "reckless disregard for the truth" is often hard to explain or grasp. Some courts are more stringent than others when deciding what it takes to meet these standards. A judge or jury typically expect to see that the thrust of the allegations involve the defendant "cheating" the government. It is important not to forget that judges and juries are ordinary people; and before they force a company to pay triple damages they may need to think that the company actually knew that its conduct was wrong. Therefore, a judge might improperly substitute the definition of fraud for the slightly lesser standard of the statute. Therefore, it is safest to examine your allegations through the lens of whether the company committed fraud in the ordinary sense of the word. Besides, if you prove fraud, you'll clearly be able meet the standard required of the DOJ Reward Program.

Waste is Not Fraud

As you might imagine, there is difference between fraud, which must be shown to receive a reward, and wasteful spending, which is not covered by the DOJ Reward Program.

The difference can be illustrated like this. If a company tells the government that it costs $700 to make a toilet seat and the company actually spends $700 to design and make it, then that is wasteful. It represents an unwise purchasing decision by the government. Although the government would do well to avoid waste, no reward is available under this program. But, if the company tells the government that it costs $700 to make the toilet seat and then goes out and buys it at the hardware store for $25, the company has deliberately defrauded the government by $675 per toilet seat. If you were to report this situation, you may well receive a DOJ Reward Program.

Funds are Forfeited

This *F Factor* is often overlooked, and is crucial to your hopes of receiving a meaningful whistleblower reward.

Whistleblowers receive a percentage of the *actual recovery* in the case. That means that if the amount DOJ recovers from a wrongdoer is small, your reward will be small. Conversely, as the amount DOJ collects grows, so does your reward. In fact, there is no cap on the amount of a reward. Some whistleblowers have received $100 million because DOJ recovered six times that amount from the defendant. To obtain a $2 million reward, you can expect that the defendant will have to repay DOJ $10 million.

No matter how good the case may appear on paper, if the government does not collect any funds, you won't get a reward. Suppose Mary files a *qui tam* alleging that Company X overcharged Medicare by $10 million. After a fierce, three-year legal battle, the Court ultimately issues a judgment for $30 million (due to triple damages). Then Company X files for bankruptcy and goes out of business without any assets left. Even though there was a judgment for $30 million, the government is unable to recover the money, so Mary would not receive a reward. While this may seem like this would be a huge hurdle, fortunately, it happens less than one might imagine. Only two or three times during the 15 years I worked at DOJ did a company file for bankruptcy in one of the cases I worked on. Even in those instances, the government was able to recover millions of dollars back during the bankruptcy proceedings, and was pleased with the result. And, yes, of course, the whistleblower received a fair share of the recovery.

It is worth remembering, however, that the biggest issue generally is not the ability of the defendant to repay the funds, but almost always the strength of the evidence proving fraud. While resources are a factor, the clearest way of gaining DOJ's attention and recovering a reward is to show that the company knew it was cheating.

Typically, if a company has financial issues, DOJ negotiates a settlement with them short of forcing them out of business. In the hypothetical, if Company X agreed to pay $1 million, based upon its ability to pay, Mary would receive between 15 to 25 percent of the $1 million. Her reward would approach a quarter of a million dollars. Of course, if they can negotiate a higher amount, her reward increases. DOJ is aware that companies often cry poverty, and has auditors review their finances and determine how much they truly can afford to pay.

Alleging Damages

The final *F Factor* raises an important practice pointer in developing a damage model. The government is very interested in how much you think the company cheated and expects to see a detailed damage calculation. After all, you are the one alleging that there was fraud. Are you able to quantify it or point the government in the right direction? Avoid making one of the biggest mistakes of overlooking the importance of addressing damages in your complaint and other submissions to DOJ.

DOJ will think twice about taking a case that *either* does not allege significant damages or overstates damages. Not providing any damage calculation can backfire too. Whether or not you allege damages, you can expect DOJ to ask you to estimate damages and to support your calculations long before it makes a decision about your case. Your best bet is hiring an experienced *qui tam* attorney that will develop a sound damage model and work with DOJ in determining the amount of the fraud.

Magnitude Matters

Be mindful that if DOJ perceives your case as a small dollar suit, it may not be received with excitement. Therefore, not only does this *F Factor* affect the size of the reward, it directly affects whether there will be a reward at all. If DOJ does not view your case worthy of expending its limited resources, expect the government to decline to take your case. Don't expect DOJ to spend $100,000 litigating a case where it recovers $100,000.

On the other hand, don't let an attorney persuade you to claim the case is worth millions, when it obviously is not. Only inexperienced attorneys think they can fool DOJ into chasing after small cases by pretending they are large. In the process, you lose total credibility by overstating the case. If DOJ cannot trust your allegations of damages, why would you expect them to believe your allegations of fraud? It is very hard to earn back lost trust.

Statute of Limitations

There is another limitation you should know about. The False Claims Act contains a statute of limitations that bars allegations that are older than ten years. In some instances, the limitation is only six years. If your claim is older than the applicable statute of limitations, the company will not need to repay the funds; therefore, you cannot recover a reward. Therefore, it is important to know when the false claims were submitted.

CHAPTER SEVEN
Hottest Areas of Fraud

The more gross the fraud, the more glibly will it go down,
and the more greedily be swallowed, since folly will always
find faith where impostors will find imprudence.

— CHARLES CALEB COLTON

D o you know of an actionable fraud or know where to look? The possibility of collecting a sizeable reward is certainly an incentive to keep your eyes open for fraud. But the last thing you or DOJ wants is to make an allegation that cannot be sustained.

Fraudulent bills are submitted to every federal agency. In fact, DOJ has paid out rewards to those who reported fraud at some of the most respected hospitals and drug manufacturing companies. In the United States, most major defense contractors have been sued by DOJ at least once. This does not mean, however, that fraud occurs under every contract or by every company. In addition, not everything you consider to be unethical will amount to a reportable violation.

The goal of the next two chapters is to start you off on the right footing. You will become acquainted with the types of cases where rewards are potentially available and gain valuable insights on the direction of the False Claims Act.

There are some new areas of fraud as well as regular cases where fraud never seems to stop. Whether new or old, there are significant whistleblower rewards available. Below is a brief discussion of ways companies are cheating. You'll also discover examples and checklists to help you spot the fraud.

Medicare and Medicaid

Healthcare fraud (*i.e.,* Medicare and Medicaid) has eclipsed military fraud as receiving the most *qui tam* filings each year, totaling well over 2,500 suits. Since 1990, DOJ has recovered more than $10 billion in healthcare fraud overpayments, with rewards to whistleblowers now exceeding a billion dollars. It's not likely that these rewards will slow down. This area is ripe for reporting.

Conservative estimates are that three percent of all healthcare billings are fraudulent. However, the Office of the Inspector General overseeing Medicare has recently announced that a recent study revealed that seven percent of healthcare submissions to the government are laced with fraud. Many other experts estimate that Medicare and Medicaid fraud is actually ten percent. Because Medicare and Medicaid are each spending over $500 billion per year, as much as $100 billion is lost each year to fraud under these programs.

Why is healthcare fraud so rampant? To start with, there are so many opportunties to cheat. There are 4,300 different types of medicinal drugs in the United States, and most are covered by Medicare or Medicaid. In addition, the number of medical procedures, services, or devices which are covered by these two healthcare programs are countless.

The Medicare program is like the house that leaves an unattended bowl of candy on the porch at Halloween. Each child is supposed to take one item. But inevitably, there are some who yield to the temptation of taking handfuls. Medicare relies upon an honor system and only audits about two percent of the claims healthcare providers submit. Sadly, many healthcare providers keep reaching their hands into the Medicare trust fund, helping themselves to more than they are entitled. That's why the need for whistleblowers is great.

Examples of Fraudulent Claims

Below is a bullet listing of ways hospitals, doctors, and other healthcare providers cheat under healthcare programs. As you read through these schemes, you may recall having seen similar situations occur.

- charging for tests, services or supplies not actually provided
- stating falsely how many hours were spent (*e.g.*, routinely adding 30 minutes)
- charging for tests or services not really needed (*e.g.*, routine ordering of blood work, frequently requesting a full panel of tests where only one or two are needed, or providing psychotherapy to people with Alzheimer's disease)
- lying about any work or service performed
- upcoding (*e.g.*, patient really has "bronchitis," but Medicare is knowingly billed for treating "pneumonia")
- billing for unallowable or unreasonable costs of goods or services
- overstating how much it cost to obtain an item
- billing for routine supplies (*e.g.*, band-aids, lubricants, irrigation solutions, gloves, slippers, prep kits, towels, monitors, humidifiers, oxygen [by the hour], anesthesia circuits, elbow or heel pads, masks, electrodes for ECG, and foam head rests)
- charging incremental nursing services (*e.g.*, IV starts, and stat or monitor charges)
- unbundling services billed to Medicare (*e.g.*, billing for individual tasks that really are part of one larger procedure)
- receiving or paying kickbacks for client referrals or to use particular products
- cost report fraud (*e.g.*, including unallowable or unreasonable costs in hospital cost reports)
- billing for samples of drugs the hospital or doctor received for free
- claiming ambulance costs for routine or nonemergency travel
- using unskilled or unlicensed workers
- charging for investigational tests
- disguising advertising or marketing costs as other costs

It's a good idea to return to this list from time to time to acquaint yourself with these common fraudulent schemes. Because there are so many ways that people will cheat if they don't think anyone is watching, the list is far from comprehensive. You can help the gov-ernment monitor the Medicare and Medicaid programs. The DOJ wants your assistance and is willing to pay substantial rewards.

The Greatest Violators: Pharmaceutical Companies

Pharmaceutical companies are among the greatest violators committing fraud and the DOJ Reward Program is designed to hold them accountable. If you bring a valid best-price case against a pharmaceutical company, your reward may be far in excess of the $1.75 million average.

Some rewards for pharmaceutical fraud are so large that whistle-blowers could buy an exotic island somewhere. That is just how much cheating is going on in this area. The combined recovery by DOJ in just 16 pharmaceutical fraud cases is $3.9 billion. In each, the whistleblowers received huge rewards for stepping forward.

Three primary pharmaceutical fraud schemes are:
1. Medicaid Rebate Fraud
2. Off-Label Promotion
3. Adulterated Products

These three schemes are described below. I want to remind you, however, the ways companies cheat are so varied, you should not limit yourself to these schemes.

There is so much fraud being committed in these areas, that DOJ selected an elite group of attorneys to handle some of the many multi-million dollar cases against drug manufacturers. This select group of attorneys is called "The Pharmaceutical Fraud Team." While I was at DOJ, I had the privilege of serving with this team in the fight against pharmaceutical fraud.

Medicaid Rebate Fraud

One key area where fraud in the Medicaid program diverges from fraud in Medicare is where a drug manufacturing company fails to pay required Medicaid rebates.

In 1990, Congress passed a law known as the Medicaid Rebate Statute. The statute is designed to ensure that the federal government does not overpay for drugs supplied to program beneficiaries. The law is focused upon the drug manufacturers, not local pharmacy stores.

All pharmaceutical companies want to participate in Medicaid. To do so, a company must agree to keep track of the lowest or "best price" charged for each of its drugs sold to private customers. At the end of each quarter, the pharmaceutical company must give Medicaid a rebate equal to the difference between what it charged Medicaid for each drug supplied to millions of Medicaid recipients and the best price to its other customers for the same drug. The rebates due from pharmaceutical companies are generally worth millions of dollars a quarter.

To illustrate how the system works, let's say that Acme makes a leading pain killer and sells that drug to hospitals, distributors, and local drug stores for an average of $1.00 per pill. Because of the volume of their orders, some large hospitals, such as Big Hospital Chain, only pay $0.75. Each quarter, Acme must tell Medicaid the discounted price it accepted from its "best price" customer.

For years, Acme has reported the $0.75 price it gives Big Hospital Chain. Under the Medicaid Rebate program, Acme must send Medicaid a quarterly rebate between the difference of the $1 it charged Medicaid for the drug and the lowest price of $0.75 which Big Hospital Chain paid. If Acme sells 1 million pills to Medicaid patients nationwide per quarter, the rebate owed to Medicaid is $250,000 per quarter. Acme does not dispute that it owes this rebate to Medicaid and pays it.

Here is where the fraud starts. A large wholesale chain store named Biggest Hospital tells Acme that it wants even a better discount than $0.75. It promises to exceed the orders Acme receives from Big Hospital Chain, if it is allowed to pay $0.50 for the drug. Acme tells Biggest Hospital it cannot give that steep a discount because it would have to pay $500,000 per quarter to Medicaid in rebates, instead of $250,000. Biggest Hospital is not sympathetic. It threatens to buy the drug from Acme's competitor.

To avoid this, Acme agrees to charge Biggest Hospital $0.50 for the drug by using a hidden discount. For Medicaid records, the price remains $0.75, but Acme hides the price difference by giving Biggest Hospital discounts on other drugs and making a generous "donation" to the hospital for doctor training. Acme does not tell Medicaid that its true best price was $0.50, and thereby pays only $250,000 in rebates per quarter, as before, rather than the full $500,000. This is fraud.

If someone files a *qui tam* showing that the true best price of the drug was $0.50, they would be entitled to a share of the $250,000 per quarter which Acme should have reported to Medicaid based upon the sale to Biggest Hospital. This adds up fast, especially if the fraud extends over several quarters or for years. With that kind of mentality driving the financial decisions of the company, it is likely that Acme is lying about its best price for other drugs it manufactures, as well.

Bundling Fraud

Pharmaceutical companies go to extreme lengths to disguise their true best prices. For instance, many companies offer group discounts when you buy two or more drugs. This is known as "bundled sales." It is such a familiar practice that you may have assumed it was done for the benefit of the customer. Instead, bundled sales are used in an attempt by the company to select for itself how to spread the discount over several products. This is not usually done for the benefit of the purchaser, but as a way of concealing true prices in order to minimize best-price reporting. In other words, the company wants to cheat Medicaid, and hence you and I who fund Medicaid through our taxes.

Some fraudulent programs work like this: If a hospital buys Drug X for $1.00, it gets Drug Y for $0.50. Remember, the hospitals have purchasing departments that are buying large quantities of many types of pills from the same pharmaceutical company. The hospital is interested in the total price for all drugs from the supplier, and not necessarily just the lowest price on any one drug sold. The question is, what price must the drug company report as its best price for Drug X and Drug Y?

On its face, you might assume it can report Drug X at $1.00 and Drug Y at $0.50. However, because there is so much gaming of the system, Medicare has stated that a company does not get to decide for itself how to apply discounts when multiple drugs must be bought together. Think about it this way, what if it only sold 3 pills of Drug X and 30,000 of Drug Y.

Would it be fair for the company to artificially state the price of the package deal? Again, the purchasing hospital doesn't care how the drug company identifies the price of each drug on its invoice. It is looking only at the total price paid for all the drugs. That is why the government requires a drug company to spread the discount evenly between the two products, based upon the sales volume of each drug using a formula supplied by the government. In other words, if there is a discount of $1.50 for the two drugs bought together and the volume is the same, the company must assign $0.75 to each drug instead of treating the discount as $1.10 for one drug and $0.40 for the other. If there is a lopsided volume between the two drugs, then the discount must be proportioned accordingly. This is the fairest way of determining the true price of a drug — rather than allowing a company to game the system by arbitrarily setting the combined discount, simply as a way of avoiding paying a rebate to Medicaid.

It may turn out that the true price for Drug X is $0.75 and the price for Drug Y is $0.75. The specific amount only matters if the company reports a best price for Drug X as more than the true price.

Companies have been known to bundle many drugs together in a manner that they know will conceal best prices. The fraud occurs when the company does not use the formula set by the government for spreading the discount evenly between products rather than trying to push the lion's share into the one drug they choose in order to give the false impression that one drug did not actually set a new best price.

The amount of the rebate owed to Medicaid is very significant because the best price reported was $0.75 for sales to Big Hospital Chain or $0.50 for any sales to Biggest Hospital. This scheme often results in tens of millions of dollars in fraudulent underpayment to Medicaid. The government is actively pursing these types of cases. Whistleblowers have already stepped forward in reporting that over 100 drugs have been part of this fraud scheme.

Nominal Pricing Program Fraud

Another scheme many large pharmaceutical companies engage in is misusing a nominal pricing program.

What started as a good policy of the government rewarding drug companies for helping the poor has been totally misused by pharmaceutical companies. The government knew that sometimes drug companies act with charity and basically give away pills for $0.01 each to nonprofit entities, such as clinics in low-income communities. Not wanting to punish charity, the government created an exception to the best price rules for Medicaid rebates. If the discount for a pill is more than 90 percent off of the regular price, it is considered a "nominal price." A nominally priced drug is exempt from the Medicaid Rebate Program. Drug companies, however, sometimes abuse this exception by inappropriately calling their steep discounts to large or best customers a "nominal price."

The fraud scheme works like this. Assume the regular price (known in the industry as "average manufacture price" or "AMP") for Drug X is $1.00. This is the price a small pharmacy would pay for the drug. A fraudulent company may offer a different price to large chain stores. It may sell Drug X to Biggest Hospital for $0.09 — a discount of 91 percent below the AMP.

If this were a legitimate sale, the company would not have to report it to Medicaid. In other words, if the company had truly sold its drug for a discount of more than 90 percent to one customer, it would technically meet the definition of "nominal price," despite the fact that the sale did not meet the true purpose of the statute, this is a loophole. However, the pharmaceutical company cannot generally afford to work within this small loophole, so it devises schemes that make it appear that they sell the drug for 90 percent off, when in fact they don't.

Naturally, the drug company does not want to sell Drug X to a large hospital for 91 percent off the AMP. So it devises a bundling scheme where it appears on paper that Drug X is being sold to Biggest Hospital for $0.09, but only if the hospital agrees to buy other drugs — on which the drug company does not give as steep a discount. In other words, both the hospital and the drug company each look to the bottom line price for the combined drug products being sold, but yet treat the discount as occurring in just one product.

Think of it this way, if the drug company gave the hospital a 33 percent discount on three drugs, it likely would set best prices on all three and need to pay millions in Medicaid rebates. But if on paper it treats the same sale of three drugs as a 91 percent discount on Drug A, and no discount on Drugs B and C, the overall discount would be the same. Yet the drug company would not report any discounts. The discount for Drug A would be a nonreportable best price and the other drugs would not have discounts.

The nominal price scheme is simply another twist on bundling sales. As you now know, when multiple drugs are bundled together as part of a marketing scheme, the discount must be applied uniformly between them, according to Medicaid regulations. The company attempts to avoid this problem by not shipping the drugs in the same box. Since the agreement with Biggest Hospital is secret and the drugs are not shipped together, the company denies that they are bundled and fails to divide the discount between them.

Since Biggest Hospital must buy two or three drugs to receive the $0.09 price on the first drug, the drugs are considered "bundled." When the Medicaid formula for bundled drugs is applied, the price for the first drug is really $0.25, not $0.09. Therefore, the drug is not exempt from reporting as the "best price" drug, not a "nominally priced" drug. The drug company would need to repay millions of dollars, and the whistleblower entitled to between 15 and 25 percent.

Because the Medicaid rules have been tightened in 2007, it is unlikely that this type of fraud will continue. However, a person can still report any fraud resulting from this scheme occurring prior to 2007. Many whistleblowers already have stepped forward to report this scheme.

Other Best Price Violations

Concealing the lowest sales price is the most common scheme for a Medicaid Rebate case, but there is yet another type of rebate fraud.

If a pharmacy company lies about its average manufacture price (AMP), it is cheating in exactly the same way as if it lies about the lowest sales price. This is because the Medicaid Rebate Statute has a complex formula for determining rebates owed to the states and federal government. The amount of the rebate is based in part upon the AMP. Therefore, each quarter, a pharmaceutical company is required to tell Medicaid both its best price and AMP price for each drug.

In simplest terms, the amount of the rebate is the difference between the AMP and best price. Therefore, if a company lies by telling Medicaid that its AMP was lower than it was, it cheats by the difference between the true AMP and the reported AMP. For instance, assume that Acme reports that its AMP was $0.80. However, its true

AMP was $1.00. This means that it cheats Medicaid out of $0.20 rebate for every pill sold. Just like lying about best prices, the damages add up quickly because the drug manufacturers sell so many pills.

While at DOJ, I worked on a case much like this and DOJ recovered $100 million. This is a ripe area for reporting fraud because it is hard for the government to detect absent inside information from a whistleblower. Given the potential large rewards, more and more people are stepping forward.

Off-Label Promotion by Drug Companies

Another significant area of pharmaceutical fraud is where the manufacturer promotes "off label" uses of its drugs. This type of fraud occurs when a pharmaceutical company receives Food and Drug Administration (FDA) approval of a drug for a specific use, but later promotes another unapproved use.

Drug companies seek to reap large profits by only asking the FDA to test and approve the drug for a limited area of treatment, but then promote the drug in treating other illnesses, outside of its testing and approval. Since FDA testing is intended to determine the safety and effectiveness of a drug for a particular use, federal laws naturally prohibit drug companies from suggesting alternative uses of approved drugs without going through FDA's approval process for each proposed use.

Suppose the FDA approves the drug X-cite to be used in the treatment of epilepsy. However, as soon as the drug receives FDA approval, the pharmaceutical company begins to contact psychiatrists to promote the use of X-cite in the treatment of depression. Other fraud cases where DOJ rewarded whistleblowers include pharmaceutical companies promoting a topic skin medicine or fungicide for treating diaper rash and a promoting a painkiller for treating cancer.

Sometimes, the hard part about these cases is proving that the pharmaceutical company actually promoted such off-label uses. It is not enough to merely show that some doctors prescribed X-cite to treat depression. You must show that the drug company targeted doctors and encouraged them to use the drug for an off-label use. That's where the whistleblower fits in and why they receive such large rewards. DOJ needs inside knowledge about these practices by pharmaceutical companies.

It is important to note, however, that the FDA rules do not prohibit a medical doctor from prescribing drugs outside of their labeled use. Therefore, you cannot sue a doctor or hospital; only the pharmaceutical company. Be mindful that the drug company will try to conceal its promotion of off-label uses. Internal documents often are the key to proving an off-label violation. In addition, there is one exception. If a doctor writes an unsolicited letter to the pharmaceutical company asking questions about the potential use of a drug, it may note some other potential uses. But, the letter must not be prompted by the pharmaceutical company.

If you know of such a practice, however, it is worth your time to investigate. DOJ has reached settlements in the billions dollars against pharmaceutical companies for promoting off-label use. Recently, one case alone exceeded $700 million.

Adulterated Drugs or Failing to Follow Manufacturing Procedures

An emerging area of pharmaceutical fraud is adulterated products. While you might think that this is limited to using ingredients that are dangerous, think again! The FDA has strict rules and requirements that apply to every drug manufacturer. Before a drug is approved, the pharmaceutical company must not only test the drug and prove its effectiveness, but it must establish tight manufacturing procedures and controls. Once approved, the company may not deviate from that strict process. Any changes must be preapproved by the FDA.

If a company skips steps or does not conduct each required manufacturing test and protocol, the drug is technically altered or "adulterated." In other words, if a company tells the FDA that it will use sterile labs and certain processes, then chooses not to use them because they are expensive, the drugs are nonconforming. The FDA treats them as adulterated. Medicare and Medicaid have rules that prohibit paying for adulterated products. Therefore, if a manufacturer significantly deviates from the approved process, it is not eligible to sell the drugs to the government.

Consider this example. Sleep-Tight sought FDA approval to make and sell a drug to help people sleep at night. Sleep-Tight was concerned that the FDA may not approve the new drug. Therefore, in its application to the FDA, Sleep-Tight included many exacting manufacturing checks and controls to ensure the safety of the product. It provided the FDA with a detailed manufacturing plan to demonstrate that the drugs would be made in the same manner as those tested. Based upon the submission, the company received FDA approval.

After making the drug for a year, however, the company slacked off in its manufacturing procedures to save costs. As with most medicines, the dose must be carefully controlled or the drug can result in medical complications. The executives at Sleep-Tight knew this, but reasoned that because the manufacturing process was running smoothly they eliminated some quality control steps.

Jason, a quality control representative at Sleep-Tight, complained to his supervisor when he was told to skip some quality control steps. He was told to shut up and just do his job. Recognizing the danger, as well as the fraud, Jason contacted a *qui tam* attorney and filed for a DOJ reward.

Sleep-Tight sought to defend the allegations by arguing that the drugs had worked as planned and, therefore, the government got what it paid for. It even hired a testing company to show that the drug was made correctly, despite less stringent quality control. The FDA disagreed. It pointed out that its approval was based on the drug being made in the specific manner spelled out in the application. The FDA took the position that, even if an approved drug were tested and found to contain the right combination of ingredients, it was adulterated if important testing and quality control steps were not conducted.

DOJ took over Jason's *qui tam* case and convinced a court that the manufacturing steps that had been skipped were essential. The court ruled that the drugs were adulterated because they had not been manufactured according to the terms of the FDA approval. Sleep-Tight was ordered to repay Medicare and Medicaid $200 million. Jason received a reward of $35 million.

Adulterated DME Devices

Adulteration is not limited to drug manufacturers, but also applies to durable medical equipment (DME) devices, such as motorized wheelchairs and pacemakers. DME manufacturers must strictly comply with all approved manufacturing requirements. If important steps are skipped, the DME devices are treated as adulterated. Again, Medicare and Medicaid will not pay for adulterated products, and the company could be liable for damages for every item sold. In a recent study in Florida, one-half of the DME companies did not meet the minimum standards for eligibility to submit bills to Medicare.

Of course, just as with adulterated drug allegations, the complaint must allege that the skipped steps were material and not some minor process. Expect that DOJ and a judge examining this type of a case will use common sense when deciding if the company adulterated a product. The court will not apply a strict liability analysis.

Mental Health Services

A recent study revealed that 47 percent of mental health services that were in the test sample failed to meet the minimum requirements for eligibility under Medicare and Medicaid. Most of the violations were for miscoding, such as claiming a higher level of service than actually provided. Roughly five percent represented services that were unnecessary. There have been egregious instances where therapy was given to patients who had Alzheimer's or were otherwise unable to benefit from the service.

The Second-Greatest Violation: Procurement Fraud

Military fraud was the catalyst for the amendment of the whistle-blower law in 1986. It remains the second largest area of *qui tam* cases and multimillion dollar rewards. Over 1,500 *qui tams* have been filed alleging fraud against various components of the Department of Defense. More than $315 million in rewards have been paid out to whistleblowers.

Department of Homeland Security fraud is poised to be one of the next big areas for DOJ rewards. This is because the government is now spending billions of dollars a year to protect the country from terrorism. Unfortunately, whenever the government spends funds, there will be those who cheat.

DOJ is asking you to report fraud under this important program. You can expect to see the same types of schemes under the Homeland Security program as have been seen in military fraud cases. Of course, undoubtedly, there will be a few new twists woven in.

Overview of Procurement Fraud Schemes

There are many fraud schemes draining government funding for the military, Homeland Security, and other agencies that procure goods or services. Below is a list of some of the more common types of procurement fraud:

- billing a government contract for work or parts used on a commercial contract (*i.e.*, mischarging)
- charging for services not actually rendered
- falsely stating how many hours were spent
- lying about work or service required to be performed
- billing for unallowable costs (*e.g.*, personal expenses, or excessive salaries)
- overstating about how much it cost to make or buy an item
- misstating the percentage of completion of the contract (*e.g.*, false progress payment requests)
- failure to conduct all of the required tests on items (*e.g.*, testing of only one in 10,000 instead of the required one in 100, or not testing at all)
- substituting a different or an inferior product than is called for in the contract
- concealing the true ownership or value of property
- employing sale and leaseback schemes (*e.g.*, selling property or buildings to a related party and then leasing it back from them)
- rigging bids (*e.g.*, firms agreeing in advance how they will bid for a government contract)
- submitting defective pricing (*e.g.*, inaccurate "cost or pricing data" when negotiation the price of a government contract)
- accepting kickbacks (*e.g.*, improper payments from suppliers to induce use of their products)
- failing to pass on to the government discounts or rebates
- filing improper or inflated General and Administrative (G&A) or Overhead rates
- violating a Federal Acquisition Regulation (FAR) or an accounting standard

- billing for work which does not comply with specifications
- failing to disclosed related-party transactions

As before, you may want to refer back to this list periodically to remind yourself of the plethora of ways companies cheat the government. If you can think of a way to cheat, you can be sure it has been attempted under a military contract.

DOJ always keeps a fresh pot of coffee brewing for those willing to step forward and report military fraud. Actually, the coffee is rarely fresh ... just hot and available. Consider doing yourself and the country a favor by joining in the fight against fraud. After all, every dime stolen by the companies hired to support our soldiers actually robs them of support.

The Three M's

You've now seen a glimpse of the most common fraud schemes. It's time to take action. In fact, there will always be fraud against the big "Three M's" (Medicare, Medicaid, and the Military). DOJ is asking you to keep your eyes open and be willing to come forward as a modern-day whistleblower.

CHAPTER EIGHT
Fertile Fields of Fraud

Where is there dignity unless there is honesty?

— CICERO (106–43 BC)

The DOJ Reward Program is not limited to Medicare, Medicaid, and the military. It applies to every federal contract, grant, or program paying funds to companies. As you can guess, the same type of fraud committed against the Medicare or the military is also being committed against other federal agencies that contract for goods or services. Over the years, DOJ has collected significant recoveries for fraud against dozens of federal agencies, including the Postal Service, Office of Personnel Management, Department of Energy, Department of Interior, Department of Transportation, and General Services Administration.

Because there are so many federal agencies and because the ways people can cheat are limitless, not every type of fraud can be addressed in a single book. Nevertheless, this chapter highlights many of the fraud schemes other than the big "Three M's" in which DOJ has paid significant rewards.

Use this chapter to build your ability to recognize different types of fraud. Then apply what you learn to the agencies and programs you or someone you know has contact with. The more you get acquainted with the types of fraud cases DOJ has historically taken, the better you will be able to understand the DOJ Reward Program and apply it to your particular situation.

Postal Fraud

There arc very few companies that don't use the post office. In fact, most companies have their own postal meters or determine the amount of postage themselves when mailing bulk quantities. Fraud against the post office is certainly ripe because it is essentially important an honor system that is being misused.

Companies use many schemes to cheat the post office out of postage due for mailing letters and packages. Some set their office meters to register less weight or use dummy packages for printing postal stamps that are then placed on other packages. Others lie about the size of the packages, in order to pay lower rates.

To be eligible for certain discounts and mass mailings, a package must be of an exact size. If a company knows that it is not eligible for the actual postal rate paid, it is liable under the False Claims Act for triple damages. This is true even if a postal clerk is ignorant of the proper postal rate and blindly accepts the package. If the company knows it is paying the wrong postage, it is fraud.

In recent years, a national credit card company paid the government $6 million to settle a *qui tam* suit alleging postal fraud. The whistleblower argued that the company had paid a lower rate than permitted to send out its monthly statements and other materials to customers. The whistleblower reported that the company provided false information that resulted in a lower rate. Rather than risk losing the case in litigation, the credit card company settled. A large monetary reward was paid to the whistleblower.

Postal fraud is one of the areas most easily accessible to most people. And yet it is also one of the most under-reported areas of fraud. If your company is cheating on postage, it is fraud. But, keep in mind that it is not worth filing a *qui tam* if the damages are small. If the amount is substantial, however, you may want to contact a *qui tam* attorney. Most quality *qui tam* firms won't take small dollar cases, and for good reason. The government will not chase down rumors of postal fraud, so you must meet the *Four Factors*, as well. Your attorney should be able to help you decide if you are wasting your time or if you have the type of case where worthwhile rewards might be paid.

Underpaying Royalties

Underpaying royalties has been a hotspot of fraud, and hundreds of millions of dollars have been recovered because of modern-day whistleblowers.

The United States owns large tracks of land and significant water rights, including miles out to sea from U.S. borders. These federal properties contain valuable minerals, oil, gas, or timber. Generally, the government sells the right to extract these resources from federal lands in the form of royalty contracts. Basically, the contractor is entitled to remove a resource, such as oil, in exchange for a promise to pay a percentage or royalty when it is sold.

Assume that the royalty rate for onshore production of oil is 12.5 percent. This means the oil company would keep all the oil it pumps from federal land and pay the government 12.5 percent of the amount it receives from its first arms-length sale of the crude oil to a refinery or other buyer of crude oil.

Obviously, for this arrangement to work, the company removing the oil from the land must keep accurate records of the amount of oil removed and the price it receives from selling the oil. Fraudulent schemes abound to cheat the government out of its royalties.

One simple form of fraud involves concealing the true price or total volume of the oil. More sophisticated schemes involve creating one or more subsidiary companies to buy the goods at below-market prices. The subsidiary makes a substantial profit on the resale, which it shares with the contracting company, at the expense of the government, which owns the land.

As indicated earlier, I worked on one of the first oil fraud cases at DOJ in which the government ultimately recovered $430 million from 16 major oil companies for underpaying oil royalties. In that series of cases, over $65 million was paid out in whistleblower rewards. Underpaying royalties is definitely a fertile area for reporting fraud.

Grant Fraud

Each year various government agencies pay hundreds of millions of dollars in research, educational, medical, and other grants. The three most common ways fraud occurs are:

- lying in an application to obtain a government grant
- concealing information regarding eligibility to keep or renew a grant
- spending grant money on other matters.

Some of the most well-respected hospitals in the country receive hundreds of millions of dollars in a wide variety of research grants. Over time, many hospitals become so dependent on these grants that they are more concerned with spending the entire amount of the grants, than with the research a particular grant requires.

A research assistant at one hospital observed that the hospital was shifting costs between the grants for budget reasons. She filed a whistleblower suit. The hospital's record keeping was not detailed enough to refute the allegations, so the hospital paid slightly over $5 million to settle the suit. The whistleblower received $1 million as a reward.

Guaranteed Loan Program Fraud

Agencies such as the Farmers Home Administration (FmHA), Federal Housing Administration/Department of Housing and Urban Development (HUD), Small Business Administration (SBA), and Veterans Administration (VA) have guaranteed loan programs meant to induce banks to lend money to people meeting certain federal program criteria. If the person or company receiving the loan later defaults, the mortgage holder can submit a claim to the government for payment under the government mortgage insurance or guarantee obligation. As with grant fraud, the most promising cases involve instances where the company has lied in the application or was not actually eligible for the program. The stronger evidence of fraud you can provide, the greater the chance of gaining DOJ's interest in your case.

Trade Agreement Act Fraud

The General Service Administration (GSA) works out agreements with contractors to provide supplies for all federal agencies. Congress enacted a law prohibiting these contractors from selling supplies to governmental agencies through GSA if they are imported from countries, such as China and Taiwan, that don't have reciprocal trade agreements with the United States. Although commercial companies and consumers can buy goods made in countries which are not part of the Trade Agreement Act, the federal government will not allow its contractors to do so, because those countries refuse to enter into a reciprocal trade agreement.

Discount-Big is a prime example. The popular store sells computers, printers, and ink at warehouse prices. It undercuts the competition by buying its products from China, where workers are paid pennies an hour. Discount-Big asks GSA to be put on the list of suppliers for ink cartridges. It signs an agreement which states that it will only supply goods that are made in the USA or countries with trade agreements.

At dinner with friends one night, John learns about this restriction. He has worked at Discount-Big for years, loading trucks with the supplies to take to government agencies. When he hears that no supplies can be provided to the government from China, he thinks, "That's odd, because all the ink we deliver to the government is made in China." After confirming the facts, he contacts an attorney and files a *qui tam* against Discount-Big. DOJ negotiates a $6 million settlement and pays John $1.1 million as a reward

In 2005 alone, there were two *qui tam* suits similar to John's. Both were against national office supply companies that violated this law. They used suppliers that obtained goods from China and Taiwan. The whistleblowers received $700,000 in one case and over $1.5 million in the other.

Many government contracts have clauses known as "Buy America," which require that all goods and services be made in the United States. Similar rewards are available against companies that violate this provision.

Customs Fraud

Another overlooked area of fraud against the federal government is customs fraud. There have been relatively few DOJ cases in this area because so few people have stepped forward to report the fraud. Perhaps they don't know what to look for.

A company commits customs fraud by submitting a false statement to reduce the amount of payment owed to the government on imports. The two most common ways are:

- misclassifying or undervaluing products subject to import duties
- misstating the country of origin in order to avoid anti-dumping duties.

The term "dumping" generally means the selling of goods in the USA at prices lower than that which the same goods are sold in the domestic market of the exporter. For instance, a country might subsidize the manufacturing costs of a product to allow it to be exported to the USA at a lower price. This is an unfair trade practice, which can make the cost of products artificially cheaper than products made in the USA. Therefore, there are laws which impose a special duty upon products that are sold in the USA for less than they are sold in their own country.

Suppose Zip-Imports ships furs to the USA. The duty on the furs is $250,000. To avoid this duty, Zip-Imports claims that the furs are synthetic and not subject to a duty. This would be a valid claim under the False Claims Act.

If, on the other hand, the furs were taken from an endangered species, it is illegal to import them at all. There is no import duty, but a complete ban. Zip-Imports could face criminal sanctions, but the import of furs from endangered species is not actionable under the False Claims Act. The key is that there must be a false statement to avoid paying the customs duty. Failure to pay potential criminal fines is not covered by the reward statute.

Educational Subsidy Fraud

There are many ways a college or institution can commit "educational fraud." These cases are often tricky to prove. The area in which educational fraud most easily succeeds is when a school lies about the number of current students or the eligibility of its students for federal financial aid. In these schemes, the school receives government funding based upon false information. The trouble is, it can be hard to convince the government to pursue fraud allegations in situations where the financial aid is paid directly to students, even if there was some false information involved.

Expanding Allegations of Fraud

Sometimes the fraud is committed by a company that does not have a direct contract with the government. The DOJ Reward Program captures most of the fraud schemes where the party receiving federal funds was a conduit. For instance, subcontractors frequently commit fraud against the government by supplying nonconforming goods that are used in government contracts. Although a subcontractor doesn't have a direct contract with the government, it submits bills to prime contractors who, in turn, pass on the costs to the government. This amounts to fraud and rewards are paid for subcontractor fraud. This is true even if the prime contractor had no knowledge of the fraud. DOJ frequently sues subcontractors for fraud under the DOJ Reward Program.

While at DOJ, I was assigned to investigate allegations that a subcontractor included unallowable costs in its bills submitted to a prime NASA contractor. After obtaining documents under a subpoena, it was determined that the subcontractor included ski lodges, jewelry and a host of other personal expenses in its overhead rates. When the subcontractor performed work on the Space Shuttle Program, it added its inflated overhead rates to the bill. NASA paid the prime contractor for the work of the subcontractor, which included the bills from the subcontractor. Therefore, NASA was cheated by these unallowable personal expenses. DOJ obtained a consent judgment of $10 million, and the owner of the firm was also criminally prosecuted and ceased doing government contracts.

Outside Accounting Firm Fraud

You probably have heard this litigation phrase: "look for deep pockets." Part of deciding whether to bring an action is determining whether the wrongdoer can repay the funds. There are times when a wrongdoer cannot repay all of the funds, but someone else who was involved can. There are occasions when it is beneficial to have more than one defendant because they can spread out the payments between themselves and make paying a large amount to DOJ easier to swallow.

One place to look for deep pockets is accounting or consulting firms that gave advice to a client to bill the government for amounts they are not entitled to. DOJ has brought suits against these companies because they knew that the advice given was not reasonable.

In one case, a top accounting firm paid $9.4 million to settle allegations that it knew the cost reports it helped a hospital prepare contained false claims. The whistleblower received $1.8 million as a reward. Of course, good-faith advice by consulting firms is not improper, even if it turns out to be incorrect. The key is showing they knew better, but still gave the advice.

Fraud by Medicare Fiscal Intermediaries, Carriers, and Others

Many agencies hire companies to oversee programs or contracts. Because these companies have contracts with the federal government to oversee federal programs, they are liable for their own fraudulent billings. This is especially true for the Medicare program. The government hires large companies known as Fiscal Intermediaries (FIs) and Carriers, to run Medicare and make distribution of billions of dollars a year. Sometimes, the FIs and Carriers end up committing fraud themselves. However, they are not liable for making mistakes in paying claims under the program.

These illustrations should help you understand this distinction. I've seen a FI pay $74 million for exaggerating its collection efforts in an attempt to improve its scores in government evaluations. Another time, a Carrier paid DOJ $76 million to settle allegations that it had manipulated data used by the government to judge its performance. The whistleblower in that case received $14 million.

In one of my cases, a contractor was hired to replace the heating and air conditioning system in a government building. The contract required all new parts and ductwork. However, the contractor reused old parts and painted the ductwork on the roof to make them look new. The contractor could not afford to repay all of the ill-gotten funds. However, another entity was also at fault. The government had hired a company to oversee the work. If the oversight company lied about performing its work, it could have been equally liable for the fraud.

In order to find out, I deposed the individual used by the oversight company to watch the workers. He admitted in his deposition that he suffered from vertigo and, therefore, had never climbed the ladders to look into the ceiling so he could see whether the contractor was using new or old parts. The contractor had taken advantage of the fact that the company managing the contract was not providing firsthand accountability. The oversight company settled the case within days of the deposition.

Pioneering New Areas of Fraud

These examples should get you thinking through some of the more common fraud schemes. Don't be limited by these few examples. Today's whistleblowers are often pioneers. They use the principles from this book to detect and report new types of schemes to cheat government programs. If you know of fraud that meets the *Four F Factors*, discuss it with qualified *qui tam* attorney.

CHAPTER NINE

Who Can Apply? Insiders and Entrepreneurs

Always bear in mind that your own resolution
to success is more important than any other one thing.

— ABRAHAM LINCOLN

Who can apply? The short answer is: Just about anyone can apply. You do not have to work for the company committing fraud. You can, instead, literally be an entrepreneur, making a practice of detecting and reporting fraud. Your own resolution in ferreting out fraud can bring you success. With an entrepreneurial spirit, it is entirely possible for you to become a proper whistleblower in many instances.

With a few small exceptions, discussed in the next chapter, the DOJ Reward Program does not limit who applies for a reward. In fact, the *qui tam* portion of the statute begins by saying: "A person may bring a *qui tam* action." The courts have broadly defined "person" to mean anyone. Specifically, the following three groups of whistleblowers may apply for rewards:

- an individual insider, such as an employee of the company committing fraud
- a group of insiders combining their knowledge about the misconduct
- an outsider (entrepreneur) figuring out the fraud through investigation

Of course, each person must still meet the *Four F Factors* to actually receive a reward. Let's examine each of these three groups in turn.

Individual Insiders

The typical whistleblower is someone who works for a company that is cheating on a federal contract or program. They may learn of the fraud in the ordinary course of their duties. Many have been asked to participate in the wrongdoing. They have seen the fraud with their own eyes or heard about it with their own ears. Perhaps they have read company documents that reveal it or listened to relevant discussions in meetings.

Some potential whistleblowers who have taken part in the fraud as a part of their duties at the company assume that DOJ will consider them to be a "fraud participant," so they try to downplay their involvement or knowledge. But, in fact, the opposite is generally true. The DOJ Reward Program actually values those with the deepest inside knowledge and details of the fraud. It doesn't matter that you were asked to carry out the fraud in the course of your duties. Of course, if you were the one who came up with the fraud idea in the first place, it's different. You could go to jail for that. But those who carried out the scheme are highly sought by DOJ.

The reason the DOJ Reward Program permits rewards to those who have participated in the fraud is because an insider knows the details of the fraud and can steer DOJ in the right direction. Insiders also have access to key documents and other information that is crucial in proving the extent of the fraud. DOJ always displays a "welcome mat" for insiders who report fraud.

Tom is an apt example. Due to his efforts, Tom's company won a big contract to sell a leading brand of painkiller to a chain of hospitals. When Tom returned to the office, however, he was not met with the accolades he envisioned. Rather, a person from accounting began yelling, "Don't you know what you've just done? You've cost the company $500,000!"

Apparently, his low price of the drug set a new best price for Medicaid rebate purposes, and the company would have to pay a large rebate if it reported that sale.

Tom's boss instructed him to tell the hospital that the net cost for the painkillers would be the same, but the invoice would show a higher cost. The hospital would then be given the remainder of their discount in the form of an educational grant. That way, the hospital concealed the true best price of the painkiller.

Tom was uncomfortable going along with the fraud. Eventually, he quit the company and filed a *qui tam*, reporting the fraud and seeking a reward. The case ultimately settled for over $100 million, and Tom receive a reward of about $10 million.

A Group of Insiders

There are times when two or more people join efforts in attempting to file a proper fraud case eligible for a reward. It may be that one person only knows a small piece of the puzzle and needs help from another who knows the rest of the story. Others want the comfort of a companion going through the reward application process.

In some instances, it is appropriate for there to be multiple whistleblowers. Actually, as much as ten percent of *qui tam* cases have multiple whistleblowers. Keep in mind, however, that there can be added risks by linking up with another person.

For instance, the more people you tell about filing for a reward application, the more likely someone else will decide to race you to the courthouse and file a *qui tam* without you. Second, you will need to share the reward. Not every reward paid out hits the jackpot. It may not be as much fun splitting a $250,000 reward as a $2 million dollar reward. Third, you will each have to agree to all the issues that arise before and after filing. Of course, if you hire quality legal counsel, they should recommend the best course to follow. Since differences can occur, think it through before you ask another to join your cause. You will want to talk to *qui tam* counsel before talking to a coworker about a potential case.

I once worked on a case where three different whistleblowers stepped forward at roughly the same time to file *qui tams*. Each made overlapping allegations that many oil companies were cheating on royalties under their contracts. However, the whistleblowers raised slightly different allegations against dozens of companies. Rather than fight among themselves over who should receive the reward, they combined forces. They agreed to share the reward and work together. It was a good choice. Their case was stronger as a result. Eventually, each one received a multi-million dollar reward.

Entrepreneurs

One of the most fascinating and overlooked aspects of the DOJ Reward Program is that an entrepreneur (someone who does not work for the wrongdoer but is looking for fraud) can be eligible for a DOJ reward. There are many instances where a concerned citizen suspects that a company is cheating and investigates the matter themselves. DOJ has greatly rewarded many of these efforts.

Keep in mind, DOJ is the watchdog of fraud against the federal government. It will aggressively seek to recover ill-gotten gains, regardless of how the allegations are initiated — whether they are anonymous hotline tips, suspicions from a government auditor, or a *qui tam* complaint filed by an insider or entrepreneur.

The things that matters most for DOJ in recovering funds are:

- Did the company falsely obtain or retain federal funds?
- Can it be proven?
- Is the amount of harm worth the resources it takes to prove fraud?
- Can the wrongdoer afford to repay the money?

If you can show all four, you have a good shot at gaining DOJ's interest. That does not mean, however, that there are no limits upon entrepreneurs. The statute is designed to prevent parasites from receiving a reward in cases where DOJ would have proceeded without any help.

Watch Out for the Public Disclosure Rule

The biggest hurdle for an entrepreneur or anyone lacking direct firsthand knowledge of fraud is what is referred to as the "public disclosure" rule. Some courts have limited rewards in situations where the allegations of fraud have previously been publicly disclosed.

There is some good news, however. This prohibition is only triggered if there was a public disclosure prior to a whistleblower filing a *qui tam* complaint. A public disclosure occurs only where the thrust of the fraud allegations appear in one of these public arenas:

- a judicial forum (*e.g.*, a criminal or civil case or an administrative hearing)

- an executive or legislative investigation (*e.g.,* in congressional, administrative, or General Accounting Office report, hearing, audit, or investigation)
- a newspaper or media article.

If the details of the fraud allegations were not disclosed in one of these three ways, the rule simply does not apply and you are eligible for a reward, even if you are a pure entrepreneur.

Simply put, even if there is a public disclosure, an entrepreneur still has two opportunities to fit within a recognized "exception" to the public disclosure bar. First, the rule only applies if a *qui tam* is "based upon" the public disclosure. Although this can save some entrepreneurs, the rule does not provide much protection if there has been a detailed public disclosure. It is often immaterial whether you actually were aware of, or relied upon, the public disclosure. A court will read the public disclosure and then read your complaint and decide if they are alleging the same thing. If the public disclosure was very generic or did not go to the thrust of your allegations, you may be able to bank upon this exception. This will require close evaluation by a seasoned attorney.

The greatest exception to the public disclosure bar applies to those who can show that they are an "original source" of the key information relied upon to prove fraud. An original source is someone having "direct and independent knowledge of the information" and who voluntarily provided the information to the government before filing the *qui tam* action. Most true insiders can meet this exception. The further away you are from seeing the fraud with your own eyes, the harder it becomes to meet this test.

The good news for entrepreneurs is worth repeating. You do not need to prove that you are an original source if there has not been a prior public disclosure. Stated another way, absent a public disclosure an entrepreneur is automatically eligible for a reward.

The bad news is that it can be difficult or even impossible for some entrepreneurs to establish that they are original sources of the information, if the public disclosure occurred before they filed a *qui tam*. The problem is compounded by the fact that some, but not all, courts find that a few common tools used by entrepreneurs to learn of the fraud can *amount to* a public disclosure. For instance, some courts have ruled that obtaining documents from the government using a Freedom of Information Act (FOIA) request can trigger the public disclosure rule. You would do well to ask your *qui tam* attorney to research this issue before submitting a FOIA request in which you ask for a GAO report or government audit.

The following two examples will give some insight. The first is where the entrepreneur was not able to satisfy the original source exception and the second he was able to meet the exception.

A lawyer represented a group of individuals who were harmed by a company's misconduct and fraudulent billings under a government program. On behalf of his clients, he filed a suit against the company. Unfortunately, the court dismissed the case on a technicality.

The lawyer later learned of the *qui tam* statute and filed for a DOJ reward himself, based upon what he learned while investigating the private lawsuit. The defendant filed a motion to dismiss the whistleblower, arguing that the attorney lacked the direct and independent knowledge needed to overcome the public disclosure rule. The lawyer argued that this rule did not apply because there had not been a prior public disclosure. The court, however, granted the defendant's motion to dismiss. The judge ruled that the actual filing of the prior private lawsuit had acted as a public disclosure because that complaint had already alleged that the company committed fraud against the government.

Because the lawyer did not have any original information, but only learned of the fraud secondhand while acting as a lawyer, his claim was dismissed. It didn't matter that the whistleblower himself had caused the public disclosure by filing the prior lawsuit. Had the attorney filed the *qui tam* prior to or at the same time as filing the private suit, no public disclosure would have occurred and he could have remained in the *qui tam* case.

In another case, a person owned a tract of land near some federal land. There was oil under both properties. The landowner hired a large oil company to remove the oil. The oil company paid the land owner a "royalty," which was a fixed percentage of the proceeds of the oil that it sold. At some point, the oil company was sold and another company took over the oil contract. Suddenly, the amount of royalties dropped drastically. The landowner thought he was being cheated. He also speculated that the new company was cheating other adjacent land owners.

The landowner asked another person to help him investigate the issue. That person researched public records to determine if the federal government owned the adjacent lands. It did. As a result of the investigative efforts, the private landowner was able to show that the government was also being cheated. He and his investigator jointly filed a *qui tam*.

Because the court followed an expansive rule regarding what constitutes a public disclosure, it held that the investigation had operated as a public disclosure. Therefore, the whistleblowers had to prove that they met the original source exception in order to remain in the case. The court ruled that by combining investigative efforts with firsthand knowledge, the pair meet the standard. They went on to receive a substantial DOJ reward.

When it comes to the original source rule, there are no hard and fast rules. Many courts find that original source information can be acquired by anyone conducting independent research. Other courts, however, are more restrictive in addressing this issue. The outcome depends upon the facts of each particular case and the court deciding the issue. If you lack firsthand knowledge of the fraud, you should discuss this issue with an experienced *qui tam* attorney.

CHAPTER TEN

Pre-Application Necessities

First weigh the considerations, then take the risks.

— HELMUTH VON MOLTKE (1800–1891)

Most people are a little apprehensive about reporting fraud. They may be afraid of losing their jobs or they simply don't know where to turn for trustworthy guidance. The good news is that you can talk to an attorney in complete confidence about your situation. You don't need to contact the government or bring up the issue with your company before getting legal advice. Before you make a decision about reporting fraud, you should get solid advice from an experienced *qui tam* attorney. Your attorney won't reveal your communications to the government or to your company unless you authorize them to do so. What they can do is explain the risks (see Chapter Nineteen) and help you evaluate whether you have a case that is worth filing.

What to Expect From Your Attorney

As you weigh the decision whether to file for a reward, consider all that will be required from your attorney to prepare a proper filing and follow the case to conclusion. Below are examples of the legal work to expect from your attorney during each aspect of the DOJ Reward Program.

As you can imagine, each of these tasks requires significant *qui tam* experience and skill. It will also require some effort by you, as well as staying power. You and your attorney will be earning your DOJ reward. Below are the roles of your attorney.

Pre-Filing Stage
- listening carefully to your story
- creating an investigative plan to build a solid DOJ reward application
- analyzing whether you can meet all of the requirements of the program
- helping you weigh personal risks against potential rewards
- meeting with DOJ to talk about the allegations
- evaluating who should be named as defendants
- calculating the loss to the government
- creating a custom-tailored and convincing *qui tam* complaint and statement of material evidence
- choosing where to file the case
- filing and serving the complaint upon the government

Pre-DOJ Intervention
- preparing you, as the whistleblower, for a DOJ interview
- helping DOJ gather facts and conducting legal research
- creating damage models and calculations
- meeting with DOJ to assist it in making an intervention decision

Post-DOJ Intervention
- addressing discovery issues raised by defendant
- preparing you for your deposition
- responding to motions by defendant, including "public disclosure bar" issues

Settlement
- assisting DOJ in determining a fair amount of settlement
- assisting DOJ in negotiating with defendants
- discussing settlement terms

Amount of Reward
- negotiating a fair reward amount with DOJ
- presenting valid reasons supporting increases in the rate beyond the minimum.

Selecting the Right Attorney

As you can see, the roles and responsibilities of your attorney are significant. Don't assume that every aspect of the DOJ Reward Program can be fully explained in a book without talking to you about your case. And don't expect that every case will go according to how you envision it.

Most cases take years to develop and conclude. They can take a lot of twists and turns along the way. Huge rewards require great personal investment. You'll need to contact an experienced *qui tam* attorney to evaluate the facts of your case. You can do this in privacy. You don't need to file a *qui tam* simply because you contact an attorney to evaluate your case.

Selecting the right attorney is probably one of the most important aspects of receiving a reward and minimizing risks. It can be challenging to find one that is right for you. You will want to select someone you trust, who allows you to feel comfortable asking questions. You also want to select someone you believe knows how to investigate the false claims, determine whether you have a claim, and present it convincingly to DOJ. There are many subtleties to address and pitfalls to avoid in the selection process. Your attorney will need to prepare a solid application to gain DOJ's initial interest. He will need to work closely and directly with DOJ in a cooperative relationship throughout the process, culminating in negotiating a fair reward. Be sure your attorney understands the policies of the DOJ Reward Program, the practical procedures of DOJ, and the workings of the governmental agency or program where fraud occurred.

Not only should you select someone who has significant experience in *qui tam* cases, but it is important to select an attorney you feel comfortable with. The case may take years to complete, so you will want to select someone who can realistically provide you with estimates and solid advice. You also want to feel like the attorney has your interests at heart, not just an opportunity to share in a reward you might obtain.

Don't Overlook Your Role

Don't forget, your role is very important. You must provide your attorney with complete facts, a willingness to persevere, and patience. One of the biggest mistakes you can make is to conceal important details from your attorney. The next biggest mistake is to make up information. This may send your attorney in the wrong direction. You can count on the fact that either DOJ or the defendant will find out the true facts. Your credibility is important in DOJ deciding whether to take a case, so don't conceal or conjure up facts. Remember, a whistleblower does not need to know every fact to get a reward.

Be sure to disclose to your attorney any post-employment restrictions or agreements you reached with your employer. Generally, a court will not prohibit you from filing a *qui tam* even if you signed a document as you left work saying you never will, but your attorney must know about it to best protect you. Tell your attorney any troubling issues that you think may affect your case. It's probable that these things can be overcome. If not, it is far better to find out before filing a DOJ application than years later. Expect that the true facts will come out. The company will ask its lawyers to dig for that type of information. Finally, your attorney cannot help protect you against risks he is not aware of. Allow your counsel to help shape the case to be filed based upon the evidence at hand.

The Case of John and the Pharmaceutical Company

John suspected that the pharmaceutical company he worked for was paying kickbacks to doctors to prescribe its drug over others. He was privy to meetings that revealed as much as $50 million a year was being spent on kickback programs for doctors, such as grants, meals, and free goods.

John contacted an experienced *qui tam* attorney and filled out a detailed questionnaire. In the questionnaire, John admitted that he did not know certain things. Therefore, his attorney suggested more information was needed to strengthen the allegations. Gathering the information was a risk, but, based on what his attorney recommended, John found a way. He copied internal documents that outlined the marketing program targeting doctors, printed out emails discussing the program, and collected other documents about the program that crossed his desk. These things filled in the missing pieces that his attorney needed to properly explain the program.

John's attorney was able to help him piece together and organize the allegations into a coherent statement, then gather missing information. His lawyer also researched the law on kickbacks and Stark violations, as well as other pertinent regulations necessary to establish that the company had improperly billed the government. Thereafter, the attorney filed a complaint and other legal filings needed to claim a reward. He also had a meeting with DOJ in Washington, D.C. where he explained the fraud and provided the documents gathered by his client. It was sufficient to warrant a full investigation by DOJ, including issuing subpoenas and interviewing witnesses.

DOJ entered into settlement negotiations with the defendant and recovered $300 million before having to formally intervene. John first weighed the considerations and then took the risks. As a result, he received $55 million.

CHAPTER ELEVEN
Filing the Application

The probability that we may fail in the struggle ought not to deter us from the support of a cause we believe to be just.

— ABRAHAM LINCOLN

A *qui tam* case begins only when the whistleblower's attorney files a complaint in district court. Your lawyer will need to tailor the complaint to the specific allegations you are making. It will need to tell the "who, what, why, how, where, and when" of the fraud scheme. It will also need to specify the federal contracts or programs affected and identify the false claims for payment. It will take time to draft this part of the DOJ reward application, which can be viewed in many ways as a work of art. It must contain all of the legal requirements of the False Claims Act and read like a good story that entices DOJ to join in a just cause.

Ask yourself, "What separates my case from others? Why is it worth a big reward?"

Nearly every *qui tam* complaint sitting on the desk of a DOJ attorney alleges in broad terms that the defendant committed fraud. They all suggest that DOJ could prove millions of dollars in harm merely by issuing a few subpoenas. If all you have are broad suspicions, do yourself and DOJ a favor: Don't file the case until you know more.

Quality *qui tam* counsel can help you develop the kind of information that not only states a proper claim, but inspires a DOJ attorney to participate. Don't lose sight of the fact that the cases where DOJ pays big rewards are where you jump start investigations with specific allegations of fraud.

It's More Than a Form to Fill Out — It's the Scent of a Hot Trail!

While a good *qui tam* attorney drafts a complaint, they prepare it with the mindset of how it will be received by the DOJ attorneys reading it and what response you want from them.

If fraud actually occurred, they don't hide it until the end. This not a mystery novel. The complaint must be clear, well-organized and compelling. After 15 years of reading fraud allegations at DOJ, I could separate in minutes an apparent winning case from a loser long before talking to the whistleblower or their attorney. Though there were times my initial impression was wrong, first impressions are powerful.

Remember, provable fraud is the scent that attracts the attention of a DOJ attorney. They are not looking for mere mistakes or honest disputes, but intentional fraud. If you can supply that in a good dose, don't be shy. Think about it another way. If the fraud in your complaint reads like it will take an entire career for a DOJ attorney to uncover, how do you think it will be received?

While drafting the complaint, expect that your attorney will ask you more questions. The act of preparing a legal document will focus their attention and any holes or weaknesses that surface will need to be filled. You will then be asked to read the complaint and certify that the allegations are true, to the best of your knowledge.

Preparing the Statement of Material Evidence

Your attorney needs to prepare a "statement of material evidence" in support of the allegations. This is not the same as the complaint. Procedurally, it is not filed with the court, but served on DOJ. The purpose of this document is to be a roadmap of your allegations for the benefit of DOJ. Because complaints can be formal in structure, they can lose the heart of fraud allegations. The statement of material evidence is your chance to stand out. It is where you set the tone for the case. Don't wait until DOJ calls and asks for an interview; give them the best you have upfront in this statement.

Detailed descriptions of the allegations are the beginning point for drafting a statement of material evidence. These descriptions indicate why you contend the acts are fraudulent and describe the knowledge of each potential witness. Here is where you explain why this is a significant fraud case. You should also provide copies of all relevant documents in your possession. There are few things better than giving DOJ a smoking gun document, such as an internal company memo outlining or admitting the fraud. (You should not take with you documents prepared by company lawyers, which are privileged. Although you may need to check local rules, a person is generally entitled to make copies of company business documents that are within his normal activities or duties.)

In a conversational style, your attorney must tell DOJ the real scoop about the case. The statement needs to explain why the assigned DOJ Attorney will want to invest time, resources, and energy into your case. Highlight the strength of the case, including admissions by the defendants. In simple words you need to show why this is a fraud case and what evidence you have to prove it. Your attorney should also discuss damages, and of course, without overselling your case. If need be, you and your attorney should go back and gather more information to position yourself to tell a great story. DOJ will be pleased to write the conclusion if you present a great plot.

Filing the Complaint

Next, it's time for your attorney to file the *qui tam* complaint. But where? The location of filing the complaint is a consideration. The False Claims Act allows you a choice of any federal district court where:

> the defendant or, in the case of multiple defendants, any one defendant can be found, resides, transacts business, or in which any act proscribed by [the Act] occurred.

In short, the whistleblower can choose between where the defendant is located, conducts any business or where the bad acts occurred.

In general, most *qui tam* lawsuits are filed in a federal court located in the state in which the fraud occurred. For instance, in a Medicare fraud case against a hospital, a *qui tam* is filed in the state where the hospital is located. Again, however, the law permits the complaint to be filed in federal court located in any state where the company transacts business. It has even been interpreted to be the state where the defendant submits the invoices to a government agency, which may be in Washington, D.C. or the regional locations where the agency processes claims.

Serving the Complaint and Maintaining the Seal

There are a few strict requirements your attorney must follow as part of filing the complaint. First, it is imperative that your attorney file the *qui tam* complaint under seal. Because lawsuit filings are generally open to the public, courts have provisions to enable certain types of papers to be protected, so that only the judges reviewing the case have access to them. This is known as filing "under seal." Documents filed under seal remain closed to the public until the court lifts the seal. The False Claims Act requires that you file the complaint under seal in order to give the government an opportunity to evaluate the allegation without interference from the defendant.

Your attorney will not file the evidence set forth in the statement of material evidence. This evidence is vital, but, at this stage, it will be used internally by DOJ to evaluate your allegations, not filed with the court. Instead, it is provided to the government together with the complaint.

Next, your attorney will serve the complaint, together with the statement of material evidence in support of the allegations, upon both the Attorney General, who oversees the DOJ in Washington, D.C. and the U.S. Attorney in the district where the suit is filed. The False Claims Act specifically states that you may not serve a copy of the complaint upon the defendant.

Be sure not to violate the seal by talking to anyone other than your attorney and the government about the *qui tam*. This means you cannot tell the newspapers or even your friends that you filed a *qui tam*. Some courts will dismiss a whistleblower who intentionally violates this rule. You need to be patient and remain a team player. Your silence protects the investigation.

A company that cheated under its contracts may take steps to destroy records or otherwise thwart the government's inquiry once it learns of the investigation. DOJ needs to gather enough facts to prove the case. Don't be the one who tips off the defendant and ruins an otherwise valid case.

It's good to keep in mind that, regardless of your distaste for the wrongful acts of the defendant, the fraud was committed against the government, not against you. It is up to DOJ to decide when the seal should be lifted and how to approach the investigation. It is not uncommon for DOJ to ask the court to partially lift the seal so that DOJ can talk to the defendant about the allegations. If this occurs, you must still wait for a full lifting of the seal before talking about the case. Even after the court lifts the seal and the fraud suit is publicly known, it usually is best for you to refrain from running to the press or drawing attention to the case. These tactics often cause a defendant to dig in its heels and stall settlement just so *you* will be delayed in receiving your reward.

Let's assume your attorney has created an excellent application and served the complaint on DOJ. Breathe a sigh of relief and enjoy the moment, because you will need to shift gears. The time of racing to complete a quality task is over. You now need to develop the discipline of patience. There is a long road ahead. After all, DOJ's investigation has just begun. It is now up to DOJ to run with the cause you both believe is just.

CHAPTER TWELVE
DOJ's Investigation and Decision

Nothing valuable can be lost by taking time.

— ABRAHAM LINCOLN

It's only natural to be anxious to learn DOJ's decision when you file a *qui tam* suit. It's already taken you a long time to gather the necessary information and prepare the paperwork with your attorney. You have a good idea of how much money is involved and, most likely, you've already run a few scenarios in your mind about how you might spend your reward. So your eagerness is understandable. But brace yourself: DOJ's investigation is going to seem tediously slow.

Slow, but Sure

An unknown author once penned these famous words: "The wheels of justice grind exceedingly slow, but they grind exceedingly fine." That is a great statement of what to expect with the DOJ Reward Program.

The statistics prove this point. First, the wheels of justice do grind slowly. The average length of time for DOJ to intervene in a *qui tam* case is nearly two years. But, justice also grinds exceedingly fine, with over 95 percent of whistleblowers receiving awards in cases where DOJ intervenes. You may have to wait two years to hear if DOJ will take your case. But if they do, you're almost certain to receive an award.

Where DOJ decides not to take over a *qui tam* case, they are likely to let you know in nine to twelve months. Over 95 percent of cases DOJ declines, the whistleblower does not receive a reward at all.

So, when you think about it, hoping that DOJ will make a decision quickly is like hoping you won't receive a reward.

Be Patient

It is not uncommon for whistleblowers to grow frustrated while waiting for DOJ to make up its mind. Two years is a long time. It's easy to start thinking DOJ is stalling or doing nothing of value. Therefore, they may insist that their attorney do something — anything — to force DOJ into making a decision.

As will become clearer below, trying to force DOJ into making an early decision is often the kiss of death. If DOJ is not yet ready to say it will join the case, but is forced to make a decision, expect DOJ to opt out. You may get your wish of a decision, but then face the daunting task of proceeding without the full weight of the government behind your case. Less than five percent survive this condition. Hopefully, what you learn in this chapter will help make sense of the waiting game and enable you to weather the long process.

Time Tables

The first point of confusion stems from the fact that the law provides DOJ with 60 days to make a decision about a *qui tam* case. That is true. But DOJ may ask the court for extensions upon the showing of good cause. Essentially, DOJ will file a series of motions providing the court with reasons why it cannot finish its investigation in 60 days or even 6 months. Courts regularly grant DOJ's request for more time, and for good reason. After all, it is the government that is the real party in interest in these cases, not the whistleblower. In some instances, the seal has remained in place for up to five years.

While waiting for a DOJ decision, there are things your attorney can do. They should keep informed. As long as progress is being made, time is not your enemy. Rather than simply complain to DOJ, your attorney should be asking what help he can provide, such as drafting document requests, performing legal research, and calculating damages.

You may be wondering why it takes so long. That is a fair question. As you consider what goes into the government's investigation, you'll begin to appreciate that there is ample reason for seemingly slow pace. None of these steps can be short-circuited in order to build a strong case.

The Start of the Government Investigation

The assigned DOJ Civil Frauds attorney will contact the U.S. Attorney's Office where the complaint was filed in order to discuss the particular roles of each office for the new case. Depending upon the size and complexity, the case will be placed into one of four categories:

- personally handled by DOJ Civil Frauds
- jointly handled between both offices
- primarily assigned to the U.S. Attorney's Office and monitored by DOJ Civil Frauds
- specifically delegated to the U.S. Attorney's Office.

The two offices will collectively decide the best handling on a case-by-case basis. However, under a civil directive, cases with damages under $1 million are routinely delegated to the U.S. Attorney's Offices, with assistance being freely provided by DOJ Civil Frauds upon request. A case over $1 million can be handled by the U.S. Attorney's Office and monitored by DOJ Civil Frauds. But expect DOJ Civil Frauds to remain actively involved in the larger and more complex cases. In all instances where a case is not delegated, DOJ Civil Frauds must be involved in approving intervention, settlement, or the amount of a whistleblower reward.

There is great value in having both offices involved. Each brings valuable and unique experiences to the table. Because a local U.S. Attorney's Office practices in just one geographical area, it develops deep appreciation for the local judges, politics, and procedures that may affect a case. DOJ Civil Frauds, on the other hand, oversees fraud cases nationwide. Therefore, it adds knowledge of nationwide practices and trends as its attorneys are devoted solely to whistleblower fraud cases. Combined, DOJ Civil Frauds and the U.S. Attorney's Offices make a formidable team.

Investigating the Qui Tam

Assume for the moment that the *qui tam* is worth more than $1 million and the case is jointly handled between DOJ Civil Frauds and the local U.S. Attorney's Office. Even though the fraud was committed against an agency, such as Medicare or the Department of Education, it is the primary responsibility of DOJ to investigate and pursue fraud against the federal government. The DOJ Civil Frauds attorney and the Assistant U.S. Attorney assigned to the case (collectively referred to as, the "DOJ attorneys") will begin reading the whistleblower's complaint and statement of material evidence in support. Almost immediately, the DOJ attorneys start formulating opinions about and strategies for the case. The DOJ attorneys will contact the affected governmental agency where the fraud occurred in order to appraise it of the allegations, solicit input, and request investigative and auditing support. The agency lawyers assisting DOJ will follow a similar process of reviewing the allegations and assigning available workforce. This initial phase can take several weeks.

The DOJ attorneys will interview you, as the whistleblower, and your counsel. It may take several hours, as they will ask you to explain in greater detail, not only the nature of the allegations, but all potential evidence that may corroborate the allegations. In complex cases, DOJ may conduct multiple interviews with you, spanning a few days. Your attorney will help prepare you to explain why you contend fraud occurred and how it can be proven. You will also be asked to describe the types and locations of internal corporate documents that the government may wish to subpoena to support your allegations. The more information you can provide relating to the fraud, the better DOJ can formulate a solid investigative plan.

Regardless of how strong you feel the case is, DOJ will have to prove the fraud in court. So, it cannot merely accept your word that fraud occurred. Swirling through the mind of the DOJ attorneys are thoughts like these:

- How much evidence did the whistleblower provide?
- Is it enough to warrant a full-blown investigation?
- What additional information will I need to satisfy a jury that the defendant significantly cheated the government?

- How many claims are false? Can we identify each one?
- Are damages provable by existing records of the defendant? Can I obtain them?

The process of finding supporting evidence to win a multi-million dollar lawsuit is lengthy because a court will require that each false claim be identified and an amount of dollar loss be calculated for each claim with reasonable certainty.

As you'll recall, in the case study at the beginning of this book, the first step was for DOJ to interview Mr. Jamison. The DOJ attorney listened carefully, took notes, and created a "to do" list. One of the first threshold issues is whether, assuming the allegations were true, the defendant received more federal funds than it was entitled. Therefore, DOJ conducted legal research and asked the agency to opine on whether its regulations were violated and if the defendant would be required to repay the funds. Next, the DOJ attorney must determine the approximate amount of loss to the government.

As each step is confirmed, the DOJ attorney must also calculate the amount of resources and time that must be devoted to developing the case. He will have to justify the time and expense needed for a full investigation, measuring against the priority of other cases assigned to DOJ.

Before the DOJ attorneys can make a formal intervention decision in a whistleblower action, they must seek input from the affected federal agency that was cheated, such as Medicare or the Department of the Education. For instance, if a whistleblower alleges that a company cheated Medicare by adding an X-ray charge to every senior citizen it treats, the assigned DOJ attorney will provide a copy of the complaint to the legal offices of the Medicare program and solicit their input and help in investigating the allegations.

The agency, i.e. Medicare, will provide information to DOJ regarding its program, the invoices submitted and make a recommendation regarding whether it believes a fraud case should be brought against the company. During this agency review process, the agency will enlist a myriad of its own program officials to evaluate the case, such as quality assurance representatives or other knowledgeable witnesses. The Medicare officials may need to print out a listing for

DOJ of all of the bills submitted by the hospital and gather data to test whether the allegations are true.

Expect that this intergovernmental review process will take time. New questions or concerns may arise during this process. As a result, DOJ may need to conduct additional research before the agency can make a formal recommendation regarding the merits of the fraud allegations. In other words, the legal office for Medicare will inform DOJ whether it supports DOJ bringing fraud charges against the company based upon the evidence. Only after receiving a recommendation will DOJ normally make a decision as to whether or not to take your case. It is rare that DOJ will proceed with fraud allegations if the agency that paid the funds disagrees that fraud occurred. After all, how would it look if DOJ files a fraud lawsuit and the company obtained testimony from the government agency stating that fraud did not occur?

Two things must occur before DOJ will intervene or take on a whistleblower case. First, DOJ must receive the agency's input and recommendations. Second, DOJ must determine for itself if this case will be worth the time and resources it is likely to require. This last and most important step requires DOJ to start proving the case.

The Need for Documents

Documents are the heart of a case. It is rare for a defendant to simply admit to wrongdoing and offer to repay millions of dollars. In virtually every fraud case I handled at DOJ, someone lied or suffered from intentional amnesia when questioned about the allegations. Yet, the one thing that never lied or conveniently "forgot" was the internal company documents created at the time of the events in question.

In every successful case, documents bring the defendant to the stark realization that, if these documents are taken to court, they will be ordered to repay the funds. The value of documents simply cannot be overstated.

Even then, it will take a few months for DOJ to serve subpoenas requesting the documents. Typically, the subpoena allows a company 30 to 90 days to produce the documents. Often, additional time is sought by and granted to a defendant.

Ultimately, it will be many months before DOJ receives documents from the defendant. After that, someone at DOJ still has to review and analyze them. It is not uncommon for there to be a few dozen boxes of documents to be delivered in response. In larger cases, the volume can exceed 100 boxes. At times, it can be like looking for a needle in a haystack. The good news is, DOJ will find the needle, if given enough time. The bad news is, it will always take longer than you expect.

Don't seek to cut the document process short. In fact, documents often are the best evidence in support of a fraud case.

In the case study, the internal document Mr. Jamison provided to DOJ was the catalyst that caused the DOJ attorneys to open a full investigation and vigorously pursue the case. Without it, DOJ may not have been able or willing to unlock the mystery.

However, that one document, as good as it was, would not, by itself, force the defendant to pay $70 million. DOJ had to have more proof and corroboration. Therefore, DOJ issued a subpoena, asking the company to turn over all of its documents related to cost estimates and calculation of labor cost estimates.

When the company produced over 100 boxes of documents, DOJ enlisted a team of auditors and attorneys to review them. Through slow and tedious analysis, it was able to piece together what really happened. The auditors showed the true best estimates. The attorneys saw exactly how the defendant had concealed its true prices and substituted inflated ones. By taking the time to go through the documents, page-by-page, the DOJ turned an allegation into a reward. There is not often a single smoking gun to be discovered, as there is in the movies. But it isn't necessary. In real life, with a great deal of effort and careful scrutiny, the story is usually told through several dozen documents. A solid claim for damages is built upon a few hundred company records. It may be less dramatic than a two-hour blockbuster movie. But this time, the reward money is in your hands.

Contacting the Defendant

When the DOJ attorneys have a good handle on the allegations, they will contact the defendant directly. Don't view this as a bad thing. Remember, your reward is based upon a percentage of the amount the defendants pays. The defendant will need to know of the allegations in order to begin accepting the realization that it may have to pay out significant sums.

When the DOJ attorneys first contact a defendant, it may initially consist of a letter outlining the case. A defendant will ask for several weeks or even months to put together a response. Either then or after a series of meetings to discuss the allegations, the DOJ attorneys will make an initial settlement demand. As negotiations progress, the DOJ attorneys may use a PowerPoint presentation of the proof in support of the allegations and provide details regarding damages. Expect the defendant to write letters advancing its defenses and prepare its own presentations. DOJ will need time to scrutinize the defenses and make counter demands.

The process of listening to the defendant's side of the story is slow, but important. While it may seem wasteful to the whistleblower, especially since they think the defenses are frivolous, it is always wise to listen to what a defendant has to say. Otherwise, DOJ won't be able to address the defendant's issues and concerns in court. In fact, the better DOJ can demonstrate why their defenses or positions will not be sustained, the easier DOJ will get a defendant to the settlement table, avoiding lengthy litigation altogether.

Don't forget, a defendant's decision to pay a settlement is premised upon business considerations, which were based largely on the defendant's perception of risks. It is only when the perceived level of risk and settlement demand are in the same field that it makes good business judgment for the defendant to write a big check. The managers will also need to show that the settlement was reasonable to satisfy shareholders.

When DOJ approached the defendant prior to taking over the *qui tam* case in the case study, it presented evidence of liability and a damage calculation. Although this is generally sufficient to obtain a settlement, this case was somewhat unique. The defendant could not swallow a $70 million pill quite so easily. Its lawyers believed that there was a reasonable likelihood that DOJ might not be able to prove that there were any damages. The company took the position that, even if the allegations were true, there was no actual loss to the government.

The company also argued that, in the end, it had paid the right price for the contract. Even though it had included an artificial cost for a litigation reserve, the final price was in keeping with the company's estimate, so the contract price was fair and not inflated.

Disputing this position took months of discussions and many legal pleadings and motions by the lawyers. The process of putting legal arguments to paper helped solidify the legal issues and allowed both sides to evaluate the litigation risks. It was through these documents that the company recognized that their position was not as solid as they had hoped and saw the value of settling the case out of court.

Summing Up the DOJ Investigation

Now you can see why it often takes DOJ two years just to decide whether to formally intervene or join the whistleblower's case. A large or complex case can easily push the initial investigation beyond three years.

As discussed in the next chapter, DOJ must still prove the fraud to the satisfaction of a court and engage in a formal discovery process where both sides of the case can conduct discovery, such as depositions. In one of the cases I worked on at DOJ, the whistleblower alleged that a chain of 300 hospitals routinely included unallowable costs and other fraudulent charges in its annual cost reports for nearly ten years. This translated into 10,000 separate false statements. In response to various subpoenas, the company delivered 20,000 boxes of documents. Needless to say, it took more than three years to investigate the allegations before intervention. This was just to position DOJ to have sufficient information to join the lawsuit. Again, this is before formal discovery began. It took over a year of formal discovery and settlement discussions to convince the defendant that DOJ would be able to prove the allegations at trial. It's true, they had to wait four long years, but the two whistleblowers were rewarded with $100 million for their patience.

The beginning of a case is exciting and filled with new events. You are the focal point of the budding investigation and DOJ may be contacting your attorney almost daily for a few weeks. You also will be interviewed one or more times and asked to supply more information. However, from a whistleblower's standpoint, things cool off rapidly. Once the DOJ attorneys have formulated the investigative plan, there will be many weeks or months without any new developments or contact by DOJ. Instead, DOJ will be proceeding with its investigation as explained above. That's when the waiting game begins in earnest.

As a practical matter, don't expect weekly reports from your attorney. If you have properly selected your counsel, based upon skill and personal qualities, trust that they will keep you informed when noteworthy events take place. If you sit by the phone, waiting for a call each week, you will wear yourself out. Do not call your attorney every week asking for updates or you'll wear him out too.

A *qui tam* case is, in many ways, a test of endurance. Be patient and take up activities to keep your mind off of the case. The time will go much faster and more smoothly, if you establish a proper perspective from the beginning.

In the end, DOJ will do one of two things: intervene and take the case, or decline. As you've learned, if DOJ declines, in all likelihood, you won't receive a reward. But if DOJ takes your case, you are almost assured of a reward. We will discuss that possibility further in the next chapters.

CHAPTER THIRTEEN

DOJ Accepts Your Case, Now What?

I will prepare and some day my chance will come.

— ABRAHAM LINCOLN

You have just been told that DOJ is intervening in your case. Congratulations! You are nearly assured of receiving a reward. As you know, in nearly every case that DOJ takes over, it collects funds from the wrongdoer, which is a prerequisite for your reward.

What Happens Next

Before the legal process that results once DOJ formally intervenes in the lawsuit, there is a short, intermediate stage that occurs between the few days between when DOJ agrees to intervene and formally files a notice to the court of intervention. With great consistency, nearly one-half of all cases settle in this twilight zone.

At this stage, the defendant is told that within days DOJ will be filing a notice with the court that it believes the company cheated the government and will be taking the lead on the whistleblower's allegations. The company officers know a press release will be issued outlining the fraud allegations. The company officers can now unpleasantly visualize what the headlines will read: "The Department of Justice Charges Our Company with Fraud." They also know that litigation is expensive, win or lose. It is a golden moment that can work in the whistleblower's favor, because the corporate officers must make a vital business decision: Do we want to litigate or settle? No longer is there any hope that DOJ will decline or walk away.

The seeds of this stage already have been planted long before. As DOJ was gathering evidence to support its decision, it already initiated settlement negotiations with the defendant. The parties discussed the strength of the allegations, the amount of damages, and what it might take to reach a settlement.

The reason many cases settle at this stage is simple. The company may want to minimize bad press and avoid the great expense of litigating against DOJ. Most companies realize that, once DOJ formally commits to a fraud case, it will see the case through to completion. It is a very expensive process to litigate a fraud case against DOJ. Companies are also mindful that DOJ wins over 95 percent of the whistleblower cases it takes over because it carefully screened the case during the investigative process and is satisfied that it can prove fraud.

As a persuasive tactic, DOJ issues press releases at every significant event in a case. The first press release is issued when DOJ intervenes in a case. In it, DOJ describes the fraud committed by the defendant in sufficient detail that most people would find the conduct distasteful. DOJ will also issue a press release when the case settles. It may even issue other press releases as significant events take place, such as winning a key motion. Each time DOJ issues a press release, the defendant's name is used and the fraud allegations repeated. Not exactly the news that makes stock prices rise!

If the defendant settles with DOJ before intervention, then only one press release will be issued and, while it will generally describe the fraud, it will simultaneously announce that DOJ's investigation is complete and there is no further exposure. The ending, rather than the beginning, of a DOJ fraud case make stock analysts happy.

There is one cautionary statement to be made about the level of importance to place upon press releases. It is not the driving factor for a defendant to settle. It merely provides a timing opportunity if DOJ has already satisfied the defendant that the case is strong and it is not worth defendant's resources to litigate.

Virtually every whistleblower believes at the start of the case that their case should settle quickly because the company would do anything to avoid bad press. Although it seems logical, it simply is not the case. It is the strength of the proof that creates a business decision for a company to settle. Adjust your own thinking accordingly. Some *qui tam* attorneys actually have a checklist that recommends they avoid cases in which the whistleblower keeps insisting that it will be an easy case or that the defendants will settle merely to avoid bad press. You might be thinking to yourself, "I would have thought the same thing!" It is true that most people think that a company will do anything to avoid a government fraud allegation and will quickly settle. But that is not the case. Companies know that it takes a lot of effort to prove a fraud case and that DOJ rejects most allegations. They also tend to treat lawsuits as a cost of doing business. Therefore, it's time to change your thinking. Expect that if you file a case that it will take years to complete and that any settlement will be based upon solid proof, not fear of bad press.

Many companies are content to risk multiple negative press releases. They simply issue their own press releases, claiming that these are frivolous accusations by a disgruntled ex-employee. They may even purposefully wait until DOJ "intervenes," to see firsthand whether the government really will dedicate the resources needed to win.

Settlements with companies are always based upon business judgments and risk assessments. Top company officials know the statistics that DOJ declines nearly 80 percent of cases and that 95 percent of the time the lone whistleblower will not prevail. Therefore, the governmental decision to intervene is a high-water mark for the case.

If the case does not settle at the time of intervention (or shortly thereafter), be patient. Although it makes receiving a reward almost a certainty, intervention is not the end of the case.

Think of it as Phase II. Remember, the reward amount is a percentage of the funds DOJ collects. This is the time for DOJ to prove to the court that the defendant submitted false claims and the amount of damages suffered.

Phase II — Discovery and Pre-Trial Practices

Procedurally, the case begins by serving the complaint on the defendant. The court will also lift the seal. This means you can finally talk to people about the case. The newspaper may even ask you or your lawyer to give a statement. Generally, it is wise not to make big waves. The case is far from over. In fact, if you are publicly too critical of the defendant, they may dig in their heels and delay settlement for months or years.

You will also be deposed by the defendant at some point. Expect that the defendant will ask you about the public statements you made and what support you have for them. There is little good that will come from making broad public allegations that cannot be supported. You already have DOJ behind you, so don't use the press as a tool to draw attention to the case.

One guiding principle is that in a *qui tam* case everything each party does is geared toward either knocking down a claim or defense, removing a party from the case, convincing the other side of significant litigation risks, obtaining a reasonable settlement, or winning at trial, if all else fails.

It is time to brace yourself for "fact discovery." Under the American system, there are not supposed to be surprises in civil cases. First, each side is required to show its hand by providing the other with initial disclosures of the key aspects of their case or defense. This includes DOJ, the defendant, and the whistleblower. Second, each side is permitted to discover from the other all relevant facts and documents. The parties will serve upon the others numerous requests for documents, interrogatory questions, and deposition notices. Responding to these items is costly and timely consuming.

Shortly after the complaint is served, the defendant will likely begin filing numerous motions. One concentrated effort will be upon attacking your standing as a proper whistleblower. Expect that the defendant will use all available tactics to try to convince a court that there was a public disclosure and that you are not an original source. Your attorney will need to be a top advocate to protect your interests here. Guess who will be the subject of one or more depositions? The defendant may try to take one deposition relating to your ability to meet the public disclosure bar and another regarding your knowledge of the facts of the case.

After this phase of discovery is complete, the parties will have no time to rest. Expert discovery begins, usually within a condensed time frame. Typically this includes providing reports outlining what their experts are expected to testify to at trial, followed by depositions of the experts. Generally, DOJ will hire expert statisticians and accountants to present its damage calculations. The defendant will hire several of its own damage experts, showing that the amount of loss is much lower than claimed.

After expert discovery, the next stage is motions for summary judgment, where each side asks the court to strike portions of the other side's case or to rule on particular aspects of the law favoring their positions. At this time, the government and the whistleblower are required to identify each false claim and calculate the actual amount of damages resulting from the fraud. If they cannot, the court may dismiss some or all of the case. In addition, a court may formally rule upon the standing of a whistleblower and whether he is to be excluded by the public disclosure rule.

In short, as a whistleblower, you are in the midst of a full-blown lawsuit. It will require much resolve and perseverance.

Settlement Opportunities

Because DOJ carefully chooses its cases and commits sufficient resources to them, it rarely loses a case. This strong positioning fosters settlement. In fact, over 90 percent of *qui tam* cases settle before trial.

Perhaps the risk of treble damages and civil penalties factor into the business decision defendants must make. Maybe the risk of litigation leads both sides to level heads. There are a few key events that will trigger settlement. As already mentioned, the first and best opportunity for settlement is at the pre-intervention twilight stage.

Litigation is expensive. If DOJ can show the defendant that there is substantial risk that it will have to pay treble damages, the defendant will need to make a business decision regarding settlement. A defendant may choose to cut its losses. Attorney fees can reach $1 million a month in the largest cases and $100,000 a month even in smaller cases.

The next opportune point for settlement is after the government presents its damage calculation to the defendant. Generally, a defendant will respond by pointing out errors or weaknesses in the calculation and prepare a competing damage model. As damage calculations are refined and risk assessments made in light of the opponent's arguments, each side develops a range of an acceptable settlement. Generally, the lead lawyers for each side will meet to discuss the damages, as well as the merits of the case.

Another opportunity to settle the case is after a few important depositions have been taken. Because a deposition can be used in court, lawyers for each side are weighing the credibility of current or former employees as they give deposition testimony. It provides a glimpse into what the jury will hear, as well as a good moment to reassess risks.

Although the justification often escapes me, sometimes settlement is postponed until after years of litigation. Perhaps the outside law firm representing the defendant is unwilling to recommend settlement until every stone is turned or maybe the defendant is hoping DOJ will lower its assessment of the case as the years drag on. This waiting game usually hurts the defendant more than the government. The slow wheels of the government keep grinding by uncovering more fraud or developing better damage models as time goes on. DOJ keeps finding more needles in the haystack. Although there are exceptions to the rule, complex fraud cases generally get better with time, not the opposite, as some may think.

When the final settlement stage happens on the courthouse steps or within the first weeks of trial, it's because reality has set in. The company becomes keenly aware that it will be labeled a frauddoer if it loses — not to mention having to pay treble damages and stiff civil penalties. All of this is hard to explain to the shareholders. A defendant can even be disbarred from further government work, either temporarily or permanently, if fraud is proven. A settlement neatly avoids this label.

Everyone is aware that a trial can be a crapshoot. Although DOJ wins most of the cases it tries, the amount of the judgment can be surprising. Juries are hard to predict. They may end up awarding considerably more or less than the most reasonable prediction. This uncertainty may explain why most cases settle.

If a settlement is not reached, the case will go to trial. There, DOJ will have to prove that the defendant submitted false claims and establish the precise amount of dollar loss to the government.

There are only three possible outcomes. The jury can either: (1) give DOJ the full amount sought, (2) give DOJ a portion of what it sought, or (3) find for the defendant and award DOJ nothing. The amount of your reward will be a percentage of what the jury awards.

The next chapters address the amount of reward you may receive.

CHAPTER FOURTEEN

Ranges of Rewards

---

*And in the end, it's not the years in your life
that count. It's the life in your years.*

— ABRAHAM LINCOLN

One of the questions most frequently asked by would-be whistle-blowers is "How much of a reward will I get?" There is no simple answer, but I can tell you the three separate factors that will determine the size of your reward:

- the amount DOJ recovers from the defendant
- the statutory range your case falls within
- the level of contribution made by you and your attorney.

Predicting your reward is very difficult, especially for a layperson or an inexperienced *qui tam* attorney. This book will not attempt to predict your particular award because each case is unique and very fact specific. Nevertheless, I will share insights into the process and how each of the three factors fit together.

The Amount DOJ Recovers

The single largest factor for determining the amount of a reward is how much DOJ collects from the defendant. It is the biggest ingredient because, by law, the amount of the reward must be a percentage of the funds actually recovered in the case. The amount of funds that DOJ receives from the defendant is known as the "base amount" or proceeds upon which a reward is calculated. The following example illustrates the role and importance of the base amount.

Assuming that the reward percentage is a constant at 17 percent, consider the effect of the overall reward depending on the size of the base amount (which is how much DOJ collects).

Base	Rate	Reward
$ 500,000	17%	$ 85,000
$ 5,000,000	17%	$ 850,000
$ 50,000,000	17%	$ 8,500,000

The reward amount rises in proportion to the base size. A bigger base is always better.

Let's increase the rate from 17% to 19% and examine the impact.

Base	Rate	Reward
$ 500,000	19%	$ 95,000
$ 5,000,000	19%	$ 950,000
$ 50,000,000	19%	$ 9,500,000

Did you notice that the increase of two percent in the rate or whistleblower share percentage, while not insignificant, is comparatively small compared to the dramatic rise in the overall reward for a larger base. You are *ten times better off* receiving 17 percent of $5 million ($850,000 reward) than 19 percent of $500,000 ($95,000 reward). The point is that your reward will be largely dependent upon the base amount DOJ collects.

The Statutory Ranges of Rewards

The next step is determining which level or range of rewards your case falls within. The most typical is when the government intervenes in the *qui tam* case and the defendant pays a certain amount to DOJ, either through a settlement or according to a judgment by the court. The False Claims Act states that the whistleblower is entitled to at least 15 percent, but not more than 25 percent, of the proceeds, depending upon the extent to which they substantially contribute to the prosecution of the case.

However, in certain rare circumstances, the False Claims Act limits the reward to a maximum of ten percent. Those situations arise when the whistleblower has provided a smidgen of original information, but has primarily based the *qui tam* upon publicly disclosed information. This is a backdoor way of reducing awards when the whistleblower bases much of the allegations on public information, yet narrowly avoids the public disclosure bar. While the reduction rule does get invoked on occasion, most cases I worked on comfortably fell within the 15 to 25 percent range.

Another range of rewards applies to declined cases, where DOJ elects not to take the case, but the whistleblower proceeds to prove the fraud anyway. As I have said, the odds of this happening are low. But in those instances where the whistleblower settles or wins the lawsuit, the amount of the reward increases to between 25 and 30 percent. The whistleblower, of course, must not only be willing and able to proceed alone, but must also actually collect the funds from the defendant in order to recover a reward in a declined case. Only about five percent of declined cases result in a reward, and even then, many were small dollar cases.

Regardless of which class your case falls within, the actual reward amount can vary greatly. Landing within a range is only the second step; you must still determine the precise point within the class in order to calculate the exact reward amount. Because the range is a wide ten percent variable for intervened cases, many have asked DOJ to explain how it determines where a case falls within a range. In response, DOJ Civil Frauds prepared a formal set of guidelines, which is the topic of the next chapter.

CHAPTER FIFTEEN

How DOJ Calculates Reward Amounts

A wise man should have money in his head, but not in his heart.

— JONATHAN SWIFT (1667–1745)

The actual percentage of a reward within each of the three categories or ranges of rewards varies greatly, with DOJ following a fairly loose and subjective set of criteria. When asked to describe its policies for determining how to fix a percentage within the ranges, DOJ prepared a formal "Whistleblower's Share Guideline." It actually consists of a listing of the factors used by DOJ in setting the exact percentage rate. (A copy is located on my website: www.HowToReportFraud.com.)

The most notable aspect of the DOJ guidelines is found in its prefatory remarks:

> 15 percent should be viewed as the minimum award — a finder's fee — and the starting point for a determination of the proper award.

In other words, DOJ considers 15 percent to be a fair and reasonable award for a typical case. Expect DOJ to begin negotiations at 15 percent. It is up to you, as a whistleblower, to show why your rate should be increased. DOJ lists several factors that your attorney can point to in an attempt to convince DOJ Civil Frauds to increase your rate.

At the same time, DOJ lists factors that warrant a reduction. Although DOJ won't go below the minimum statutory range, for every factor that you suggest warrants an increase, DOJ can refer to a factor canceling it out. DOJ's view is fairly strong, especially in light of the fact that the overall average percentage of all cases is 18 percent, which is slightly below the midpoint of 15 and 25 percent. How well will your attorney work with DOJ in this setting?

General Factors

DOJ's factors favoring an increase or decrease include certain actions of the whistleblower taken prior to filing the complaint, such as whether you helped stop the fraud quickly, rather than allowing it to continue for years so as to potentially increase your reward. You can also increase the reward amount if the allegations contain certain non-tangible benefits, such as ending a practice affecting safety (e.g., using unsafe or conforming materials). Your attorney's knowledge of public programs will help in this area.

The extent of your risks in blowing the whistle is also given some weight. Be sure to mention every risk factor you can. Your personal risk in reporting fraud is one of the few elements without a countervailing negative factor. Therefore, plan to put together a strong showing that you took significant risk in stepping forward.

The factors for increased or decreased awards also include aspects of public disclosure, such as how much of your case was personally known by you or based upon public information and whether or not the government already had some prior knowledge of the allegations. (You simply cannot get away from the pubic disclosure issue at any stage of the case.) Therefore, keep distancing yourself from being seen as a parasite. Let DOJ know that you are an insider truly interested in ending a fraudulent practice.

The Role of your Attorney

Many factors focus upon your role and the efforts of your attorney in the prosecution of the *qui tam* itself. This is one of the few areas over which you have direct control.

DOJ attorneys will be thinking about how much help you were when you first raised the allegations. Did you relay to the government extensive, firsthand details of the fraud to better equip it to pursue the case? The DOJ attorney will also think through how much help you gave while he was gathering support and in negotiating with the defendant. Overall, were you a help or a hindrance to DOJ? The activities of your attorney are equally important. Did he provide substantial assistance to the government?

In short, not only is your positive conduct a positive factor that can increase your reward, but any negative conduct is a distinct liability that can reduce your reward.

In the earlier case study, Mr. Jamison was given a reward of 17 percent of the $70 million DOJ recovered. His total reward was $11.9 million.

There would be many reasons why DOJ would arrive at this percent. First, Mr. Jamison would be clearly entitled to more than the minimum 15 percent because he brought forward a smoking gun document. On the other hand, he did not have more knowledge of the details of the fraud and the case settled fairly quickly. For those reasons, DOJ did not consider a large percent justified.

On the bright side, 17 percent of a case that large settled early is better than 20 percent of one that may not settle and could be reversed on appeal. Given the risk that a court could have issued an adverse ruling on either liability or the amount of damages and in light of the bankruptcy issues, the settlement was well timed.

Mr. Jamison's case illustrates that, despite the formal guidelines issued by DOJ, the process of determining the percentage of the reward remains very subjective. It is based strongly on perception. A lot depends upon the view of the assigned trial attorney with DOJ Civil Frauds. They are the ones preparing the memorandum recommending the amount of the reward. Their recommendations carry much weight because they know the case best. Therefore, the DOJ attorneys are the ones you want to convince that you and your attorney were helpful team players.

You Can Have a Role in the Process

It can almost appear that the DOJ switches from friend to foe as soon as a settlement with the defendant is reached and the amount of a reward is to be fixed. But don't fall into this thinking. The relationships between the parties were fixed much earlier. They are not beginning, but culminating here.

If you and your attorney have been team players with DOJ, you shouldn't be worried about this final stage of the process. The DOJ attorneys have already marked those factors down as positives. If, however, your counsel has persisted with antagonistic behavior or has been completely absent throughout the case, you can easily guess how that may adversely affect the amount of your reward!

I cannot state it too strongly: Your best advantage, by far, is for you and your attorney to build and maintain a good working relationship with the DOJ attorneys from the start.

Negotiating the Reward

When DOJ fixes the amount of a reward, it is not done in a vacuum. The DOJ attorneys first tell your attorney what percentage they are willing to recommend. Your attorney can negotiate with DOJ as to the exact amount of the reward. The discussions can take a few days or even weeks, depending upon the gap between the positions of the parties.

If you simply cannot agree with DOJ upon a fair award, your attorney can ask the court to set an amount. He may file a motion in district court requesting a hearing. A minitrial may be conducted, with witnesses and documents provided to the judge. Regardless of what amount it offered in settlement, expect DOJ to begin at 15 percent in the hearing. Of course, DOJ can also ask the court to rule that there was prior public disclosure and ask the court to find that the whistleblower should be either dismissed or that your reward should fall within the zero to ten percent range.

Have you heard the saying, "Pigs get fed. Hogs get slaughtered"? A greedy, adversarial tactic used against DOJ can sometimes be your worst enemy. I once saw a misguided whistleblower's attorney take an aggressive, adversarial style with DOJ.

At nearly every turn, he argued and fought with DOJ. Even during settlement discussions, he stood against DOJ's positions, despite the fact that the case had settled for $120 million! Before the settlement agreement with the plaintiff was signed, the whistleblower's attorney filed a motion asking that the court hold in escrow 25 percent of the proceeds for the whistleblower. The insulting implication was that he did not trust DOJ to pay the reward. By reserving 25 percent, the attorney also made it clear that he intended to demand a full 25 percent of the proceeds. The attorney knew that DOJ was unlikely to offer a 25 percent reward, since the case had settled quickly. So he resorted to a hardball tactic to try and gain leverage for a larger reward.

Because they filed a motion, DOJ had to respond with a legal brief to the court. While conducting legal and factual research for the brief, DOJ attorneys were able to show that the whistleblower did not have personal knowledge of each of the claims being settled and that there had been a prior public disclosure of the allegations. As a result, DOJ filed a motion to exclude the whistleblower from a large portion of the settlement.

At the end of the day, the parties settled the issue and the whistleblower was paid $12 million, which was roughly ten percent of the settlement. Although this is not a bad amount, the normal minimum 15 percent would have yielded $18 million, and a somewhat more average 18 percent would have been $21 million. If the whistleblower and his attorney had been team players and not filed a motion to try to force DOJ into paying 25 percent, who knows what they might have received?

Summary

Whether, when, and how much of a reward a whistleblower may receive depends upon a lot of factors. It's hard to predict the amount of a reward you might receive. Before you get involved in trying to guess what amount you might receive, make sure you have answered two of the most immediate and important questions:

Do you have the type of case that may receive a reward at all?

Can your attorney present your case to DOJ in an effective manner?

Let these be your first considerations. If you fail to become eligible for a reward, the ranges of awards have no meaning.

CHAPTER SIXTEEN
Why DOJ Rejects Cases

> *My greatest concern is not whether you have failed,*
> *but whether you are content with your failure.*
>
> — ABRAHAM LINCOLN

Before explaining some of the reasons why DOJ rejects so many applications, allow me to dispel a common misunderstanding.

Some people mistakenly believe that, because DOJ rejects close to 80 percent of all whistleblower reward applications, DOJ must not be aggressively pursuing fraud. Nothing could be further from the truth. The Civil Fraud Section of DOJ, the office responsible for the DOJ Reward Program, is staffed by some of the most intelligent, hard-working lawyers in the country.

To put some teeth behind this statement, consider that each year the Civil Fraud Section receives hundreds of unsolicited resumes from attorneys working at prestigious law firms. The director of the Fraud Section not only has the luxury of being particular over those she hires, but can afford to limit the selection to those who have a deep desire to combat fraud.

These same DOJ Civil Frauds attorneys, combined with the Assistant U.S. Attorneys nationwide, are collecting over a billion dollars a year under the whistleblower program. These figures make it hard to argue that DOJ attorneys are not hardworking and aggressive.

The DOJ attorneys take their roles and responsibilities very seriously. Not only do they receive intensive fraud investigative training when they start, but the internal training never stops. Each quarter, DOJ Civil Fraud attorneys meet to discuss current trends and changes in the law. Almost daily these DOJ lawyers communicate with one another by email to share new approaches and tactics in particular cases. The DOJ attorneys also report regularly to supervisors to talk strategy. In turn, the supervisors meet together weekly and with the director to ensure the cases are progressing and discuss trends. Those DOJ attorneys with similar cases also meet to discuss approaches, as well as better ways to investigate and pursue cases.

DOJ also has a myriad of internal tools addressing most procedural and substantive issues affecting its reward program. The performance of each DOJ attorney is also constantly measured through quarterly reports and annual reviews. In short, the DOJ Civil Frauds office is a well-oiled machine. If a whistleblower advances a case that has merit, you can count on DOJ vigorously investigating and pursuing it.

Why DOJ Declines Cases

So why do so many cases get rejected? DOJ won't publicly comment on the reasons why it declines a particular case. This only makes sense. If DOJ did, defendants would be able to get access to the internal DOJ memoranda explaining the investigative efforts and findings. In other words, before DOJ declines a case, its attorneys prepare a detailed memorandum explaining the allegations and the reasons why DOJ should not take the case. This is a roadmap of the internal government thinking of the case, complete with frank discussions of the evidence and policies.

This memo is protected from disclosure under various privileges similar to the attorney-client privilege. The harm of sharing the manner in which DOJ investigates cases can have a much larger impact than simply the case itself. Some unscrupulous contractors may use this information to help figure out ways to circumvent the law or a government investigation in the future. Also, if the DOJ states that there is insufficient evidence of knowledge by the defendant, publicly producing it will kill any chance for the whistleblower pursuing the declined case on their own.

Can you imagine a whistleblower pursuing a declined case knowing that a jury will read a DOJ memo stating that it does not have confidence that a fraud case can be proven?

In some cases, however, protection from disclosure privileges can be waived. For instance, if the government publicly discusses its deliberative process, it may not be able to withhold the internal memo. If there is a waiver, a company will also seek to depose the DOJ attorneys asking them to produce every critique they made of witnesses and evidence. This would be disastrous and make it virtually impossible for a whistleblower to continue with the case. For instance, if the internal DOJ attorney memo discussed all of the reasons why it would be hard to prove fraud, the defendant would show the memo to the jury. Even if subsequent discovery demonstrates that fraud did in fact take place, the defendant would still tout the memo.

Of course, an inability to prove fraud is not the only reason why DOJ may decline. It may have little to do with the merits, and may turn to the fact that DOJ does not have resources to take every case. DOJ's standard response in a declined case is that the act of declining does not mean it thinks the case lacks merit. In fact, DOJ points out that it can decline a case based upon factors such as lack of resources, amount of money likely to be involved, or the facts of a particular case. Below is a brief discussion of these three reasons.

Resources

Not every agency is able to assign investigators for every case. Remember, there are many new *qui tams* filed each year. Certain judgments must be made upon the potential merits of a case. That begins with how specific the complaint is regarding the scope of the fraud and how well it is presented to DOJ. Certainly every *qui tam* gets a fair shake, but obviously some deserve and receive more attention than others. Rather than stew about this fact, hire quality *qui tam* counsel and present your case in a manner demonstrating it is worthy of the time and resources necessary to win a big fraud case.

Amount of Money

A common problem with many *qui tam* complaints is that they fail to show any actual loss or damages to the federal government. Most simply say that the loss is in the millions or that it is substantial. Very little effort or time, however, is spent on discussing precisely how the government was actually harmed and how this harm can be quantified.

This deficiency is likely to be the result of the whistleblower's attorney being unfamiliar with government contracts or programs and, as a result, not knowing how to calculate the loss.

Often, inexperienced *qui tam* counsel bring fraud cases to DOJ in which there are little or no damages to the government. The whistleblower is chasing a dead end.

Think about this issue in another way: If you cannot provide evidence of specific damages, what amount of reward do you hope to receive? Fifteen percent of nothing is nothing.

The Facts of the Case

There are a variety of reasons why the facts may warrant DOJ turning down a case.

First, the facts are often just flat out insufficient to state a claim.

Second, a significant problem with many cases is that they do not show that the defendant knew the claim was false. Absent guilty knowledge, there is no violation of the Act. Innocent mistakes and honest disputes simply are not actionable under the False Claims Act. Remember, statute is *fraud based.* It does not cover every situation where there is a mere overpayment. The government needs and depends upon your inside information. Don't file a *qui tam* without it.

Third, many applications also fail to meet one or more of the procedural and substantive requirements of the False Claims Act, such as failing to allege a required element of the law in the complaint or failing to plead the details of the fraud, such as the who, what, where, when, and why? If the complaint does not set forth allegations that establish fraud, how much weight should DOJ give it? The cure is to enlist qualified *qui tam* counsel before filing suit, someone who can identify what is missing and create a plan for obtaining it.

Last, a remarkable number of *qui tams* look as if they have been slapped together without careful thought or examinations. If the complaint your attorney drafted is obviously a pastiche of generic allegations, why would you expect DOJ to put two years of effort into something you and your counsel didn't care enough about to tailor to the case at hand? Similarly, a poorly worded complaint cannot help but give DOJ the impression that the underlying facts and allegations most likely reflect the same slipshod quality. There are many *qui tams* filed each year fighting for the attention of DOJ Civil Fraud lawyers. It is inevitable the DOJ attorneys will take most seriously the *qui tams* that are obviously professional, well-informed and thoroughly prepared.

Unproductive Areas

Although not speaking for DOJ, I am averse to several types of allegations.

Civil Penalty Cases

The first unproductive area consists of cases in which a technical violation is alleged without any actual loss to the government.

The False Claims Act requires that the defendant in a fraud case be required to pay "civil penalties" of between $5,500 and $11,000 per false claim submitted, even if there is no loss to the government. The imposition of penalties is not discretionary, but mandatory.

An inexperienced *qui tam* attorney can see this as an opportunity. It relieves the whistleblower of proving damages in cases where loss to the government is nonexistent or difficult to prove. As long as the attorney can prove that numerous false claims have been submitted, the dollar values of the case can rise enough to merit consideration.

These attorneys mistakenly assume that if they merely show something was wrong with an invoice, the government will collect up to $11,000 per violation. A simple trail of paperwork would be enough to provide evidence of false invoices. Fraud and intent are much more difficult to prove.

Experienced *qui tam* counsel do not make this mistake. They know that, even in cases where there is some harm, they cannot reasonably expect a court to award millions of dollars in penalties.

In one case I oversaw at DOJ, a whistleblower ran to the press declaring that he had uncovered a billion-dollar fraud scheme. Based upon simple mathematics of counting every invoice the group of hospitals submitted to Medicare and multiplying it by $11,000, he and his attorney had arrived at a $1 billion figure.

The declaration was sufficiently dramatic that the press printed a front-page headline the next day, stating that the hospitals had cheated

Medicare by a billion dollars. As you might guess, the defendants were extremely upset. Now they had to defend against the damage to their reputation, as well as the government's complaint. The whistleblower's rash claim had suddenly made it important for the hospitals to call in the big guns. They hired several prominent law firms and litigated for six years before finally agreeing to a settlement.

The case eventually settled for $2.75 million, which was much closer to the amount of actual loss. The whistleblower received $750,000. While it was not a bad reward, it was a rude awakening for the whistleblower who thought he might receive over $100 million based upon civil penalties. The inflated view of the case was also the primary reason for the delay of six years in receiving a reward.

In short, if there are no damages or little actual loss to the government, a court will be reluctant to award significant penalties.

Environmental Violations

The second type of case I find unfruitful is when a person alleges that a company has concealed its violation of a law to avoid paying a criminal fine.

The argument goes something like this. If a company had told the government it was not complying with environmental laws, the EPA would have issued a fine. The damage sought is the hypothetical EPA fine the company avoided paying by not reporting its own wrongdoing. These cases are not only disfavored by me, but by most courts.

This type of case should not be confused with those where a contractor has specific contract obligations relating to environmental compliance, such as the management of a Department of Energy facility. A proper case can be made if the company has a duty to report the information as a condition of payment, but fails to do so and harm comes to the government as a result. Perhaps bonuses have been given to the contractor, based upon the mistaken belief that they were in compliance.

While at DOJ, I took one of those cases to trial, proving that a company had lied about its environmental performance in order to receive these types of bonuses. The court ordered the contractor to return $4 million in award fees. But I have never joined a whistleblower case that merely alleged that fines were avoided by failing to report a problem.

Government Knowledge Cases

Another unproductive area for a whistleblower occurs in situations where there existed government knowledge at the time of the invoice. For instance, the government may have been aware of the true nature of the goods or services being delivered and knowingly waived a defect.

Suppose the contract required a contractor to make missile drones for target practice for pilot training. During production, the contractor notified the contracting officer that the speed of the drones was not within the contract specifications due to the size engines and design called for in the contract. Together, the military and the contractor worked towards a solution that was ultimately acceptable to the government.

Thereafter, a whistleblower filed a *qui tam*, alleging that the drones did not meet the specifications and that the contractor knew they were out of tolerance. The court dismissed the *qui tam* suit because the contractor did not knowingly submit false statements because it had fully disclosed the problem and worked with the government as to an agreed upon solution.

The key to the government knowledge defense is that a defendant must make full disclosure of the problem and follow the advice of the government. It is not sufficient merely to say that the government knew of the problem. For instance, a contractor is still liable under the False Claims Act if it calls up a contracting officer and says, "I know that I am suppose to use a 5 hp engine, but am only going to use a 4 hp engine." Only if the government agrees to allow a substitution will the contractor avoid liability.

A variation includes situations where the government learns of the defect after payment but states that even if it had known at the time of payment, it would have still paid the invoice. In both situations the goods or services provided may not technically comply with the contract specifications, but the government is happy with the product. In other words, even if it had known the truth at the time, it would not have made a difference.

Although government knowledge is not *per se* a defense, most courts require that the false claim must be material to the payment of funds. If the government would have paid the claim anyway, there may be no real harm to correct. Before intervening in any *qui tam*, DOJ will contact the agency and ask if it knew of the allegations at the time and agreed to pay the funds anyway. DOJ will similarly ask the agency if it had known the truth at the time, would it have still paid the funds. It is rare that DOJ will pursue a fraud case that the agency is not willing to support.

CHAPTER SEVENTEEN

What are Your Options if DOJ Declines?

Take calculated risks. That is quite different from being rash.

— GEORGE S. PATTON (1885–1945)

DOJ turns down three out of four *qui tam* cases. Of course, if DOJ declines your case, you'll find little comfort in knowing that you are in the majority.

The program does, however, give you the option of going forward without DOJ. If you do, it means you will be required to prove to the court that the defendant cheated the government and to establish the amount of loss. Your attorney will have to litigate against the defendant without the help and resources of the government. That means he must front the entire cost of the case, including document productions, depositions, and filing motions. This can range between tens of thousands of dollars to over a million dollars.

If you succeed, the majority of the judgment against the defendant will go to the government. You will receive at least 25 percent of the amount the court awards the government, but no more than 30 percent. The government will get roughly 75 percent of the amount you recover for it. Nonetheless, if the amount of recovery is large enough, it can be a worthwhile adventure, provided you are up to the challenge.

If DOJ declines, you and your lawyer face a difficult decision. Should you proceed without the government or fold up your tent? If you decide to quit, all you have lost is your time, assuming it is a contingency case. If you decide to go forward, you will do so knowing that the odds of recovery are extremely low and you will not have the benefit of DOJ resources.

If you and your attorney believe strongly enough in your case, you may decide to go forward anyway. Before making that decision, however, there are some additional risks to consider.

Rewards Are Not Very Likely

In roughly 95 percent of cases where DOJ does not intervene in, whistleblowers do not receive a reward. That means that your odds of recovering a reward slipped from about 25 percent, when you first filed the case, to less than five percent.

Yet, this statistic doesn't tell the whole story. It need not be the deciding factor in whether you proceed.

This figure represents 95 percent of the cases in which DOJ declines to intervene, it does *not represent* 95 percent of the cases pursued by whistleblowers on their own.

In most instances, a whistleblower automatically withdraws the case the moment DOJ declines. Because the vast majority of cases are voluntarily dropped, the 95 percent number is skewed. Unfortunately, there are no statistics regarding the percentage of declined cases that are actively pursued that lead to a good result. My experience is that most of the declined cases that settle are for low amounts, with rewards far below the national average. Only a small percent of declined cases result in a very large recovery.

Your decision to proceed with a declined case needs to be based upon the strength of your allegations and the ability of your attorney to proceed against the defendant.

Risk of Paying Attorney Fees and Costs

The whistleblower law provides that, if the government declines to intervene and the whistleblower still proceeds with the case, the court may award the defendant reasonable attorneys fees and expenses — under one of two conditions.

That's right, in a declined case, the whistleblower might be ordered to pay the defendant its attorney's fees.

The first condition is that the defendant must actually win the case. This can occur if you cannot meet the burden of proof that there was actionable fraud or if they convince a court to dismiss the case under the public disclosure bar.

The second condition is that the judge must find that your claim was "clearly frivolous, clearly vexatious, or brought primarily for the purposes of harassment." Fortunately, it is not enough that you simply lost the case or relied upon some new or novel theory. The defendant must show that you had an improper motive in forcing the defendant to defend a frivolous case.

Even though the law clearly provides for the possibility, a finding that the plaintiff must pay the defendant's attorneys fees and costs in these cases are somewhat rare. However, it is not unheard of.

In one case, the court awarded costs against a whistleblower who had previously filed a copyright suit against the defendant and lost. The court determined that the *qui tam* was essentially a re-litigation of the prior suit and, as such, it qualified as harassing and vexatious.

In a case I declined while at DOJ, the court required the whistleblower to personally pay $75,000 for pursuing frivolous issues. The whistleblower had continued to press the case on appeal, even after the judge had ruled that the whistleblower failed to prove any false claims. The whistleblower could not give up the sinking ship and kept filing motions after it was clearly futile. Had the court decided to assess costs for the entire case, the whistleblower would have been liable for considerably more than $75,000. Fortunately for him, the court was merciful and only held him responsible for the defendant's costs in responding to the final appeal.

It is worth re-emphasizing that this "cost" provision does not apply when the government intervenes. It also does not apply when the whistleblower drops the case right after the government declines. This helps explain why so many whistleblowers dismiss the suit immediately after the government opts out. That way, whistleblowers never risk paying any costs. As you can see, given the rate charged by big firms representing defendants, being assessed costs can easily amount to sums exceeding your annual income.

DOJ Attorneys are Not Likely to Change Their Minds

If you proceed in a declined case, you can always ask DOJ attorneys to change their minds later and get back into the case. The law provides that DOJ can move to intervene at *any* stage. Although this is an option, don't count too highly upon it occurring.

In 15 years at DOJ, I only changed my mind once after declining. Very few others in DOJ Civil Fraud changed their minds either. But it does occur on occasion, so there is no harm in asking DOJ to reconsider, if you proceed with a declined case.

Reward Percentages Increase

The silver lining to proceeding with a declined case is that if you do obtain a settlement or win at trial, you will receive between 25 and 30 percent of the recovery. If you have a good claim but DOJ for some reason doesn't accept the case, you may still convince the defendant to settle, which will save you the costs of trial.

When a whistleblower does continue to pursue a case, even after DOJ declines, one of the most common reasons is because the whistleblower was fired or forced out of a company for threatening to blow the whistle. Retaliation can be a compelling motive that keeps whistleblowers going, despite the risks.

Often, whistleblowers in those situations proceed with the declined case and simultaneously file a wrongful termination claim. The defendant is far more inclined to settle a case when the whistleblower can show that they were fired because of their concern that the company might be committing fraud against the government.

The Final Analysis

That said, there are some compelling reasons to drop the case when DOJ declines.

Without DOJ in the case, for instance, the whistleblower becomes the center of attention. The defendant will do everything in its power to dismiss you from the case. Expect that the defendant will tell the court over and over again that the government declined because there was no case, so the court should similarly dismiss it. You may even be characterized as a rogue or disgruntled employee, who lacks credibility and is simply in it for the money.

Although most whistleblowers decide not to pursue the case if DOJ declines, there are success stories. The largest recovery in a declined case was over $100 million, and the whistleblower received a share of over 25 percent. Given the right conditions, you may choose to litigate without DOJ on your side. But you will need a tough skin and an attorney with deep pockets.

In the end, this type of decision is best made with sober judgment and solid input from your attorney.

CHAPTER EIGHTEEN
Attorney Fees and Tax Issues

Lawyers are ... operators of the toll bridge
which anyone in search of justice must pass.

— *Jane Bryant Quinn*

Attorney Fees and Contingency Rates

Because *qui tam* cases often take years to complete and there is no guarantee of a reward, the most common way to hire an attorney is to agree to give them a percentage of the reward. This is known as a contingency fee.

The rate of contingency fees, however, varies greatly. Although *qui tam* attorneys generally don't publicize their rates, expect the rate for *qui tam* cases to be between 40 to 50 percent of the amount of a reward paid to a whistleblower. A few firms have been known to charge as high as 60 percent.

While the rate certainly affects how much you will receive, you should not select your *qui tam* attorney based upon the lowest rate charged. Any attorney can hold himself out as qualified to do virtually any area of the law, whether it is personal injury, antitrust law, or *qui tam* work. You will want to inquire into their background and experience. Conversely, do not make the mistaken assumption that the firm with the highest rate is better than one charging a more average rate. Most people tend to associate cost with value, but this assumption is not always justified.

What you may not know about attorney fees is that the whistle-blower program permits your lawyer to collect from the defendant their attorney fees and costs incurred in the case. These fees will not reduce your DOJ award. They are collected by your lawyer directly from the defendant over-and-above the base amount DOJ recovers from the defendant. In other words, after a defendant pays DOJ a settlement amount, your lawyer will bill the defendant an additional amount for fees and costs. These fees are in addition to the contingency rate you pay your lawyer from the reward. Don't expect to get a portion of these fees. They go to your attorney and are not part of the contingency arrangement. Your reward consists of the amount DOJ pays you, less the contingency fee percentage paid to your lawyer.

Don't begrudge these additional fees your lawyer receives from the defendant. Your attorney will be battling against some of the largest and best law firms in the country. As Abraham Lincoln said, "A lawyer's time and advice are his stock in trade." By taking your case, your attorney is giving up the opportunity to work on other matters at his normal billing rate. Considering that DOJ declines 80 percent of all cases, he is risking much to take your case. In addition, included in these costs are amounts of out-of-pocket expenses incurred, such as deposition fees and outside consultants and experts. In a normal case, the client would bear these costs.

IRS Form 1099 and Tax Consequences

What are the tax consequences of receiving a DOJ reward?

Not surprisingly, a whistleblower reward is taxable income. Whenever DOJ pays a reward to a whistleblower, it issues to the whistleblower an IRS Form 1099. DOJ lists the full amount of the reward it paid out under the case. The form is also sent by DOJ to the IRS listing the whistleblower as the recipient of the reward.

In 2003, the IRS ruled that, although the entire amount of the reward was income, the taxpayer could not deduct the lawyer's contingency fee. This ruling was appealed.

In 2004, the Second Circuit Court of Appeals stunned the legal profession by upholding the IRS's position that the whistleblower must pay tax on the full amount of the award, despite the fact that her attorney received a substantial contingency fee from the reward. In the case in question, DOJ paid the whistleblower $900,000, of which the whistleblower gave $300,000 to his attorney. Even though she only received $600,000, the IRS required her to pay taxes on $900,000 and the court upheld that requirement.

Almost immediately after this decision, Senator Chuck Grassley of Iowa proposed a law that would permit whistleblowers to deduct the contingency fees from their income. On October 22, 2004, Congress passed this new, more equitable law, which overrides the IRS regulations.

The good news is that, today, a whistleblower is able to deduct from income the amount of the contingency fees. Only the amount the whistleblower receives after paying the contingency fee to her attorney is taxable income.

Because tax issues are complex and subject to change, it is a good idea to contact an experienced tax accountant or advisor before relying on any regulations that have been true in the past. This is something you can typically wait to do until a settlement is imminent and your attorney is negotiating an amount of the reward with DOJ.

CHAPTER NINETEEN
Personal Risks for Reporting Fraud

Great deeds are usually wrought at great risks.

— HERODOTUS (484–430 BC)

Before filing a *qui tam* is the time to assess whether the potential rewards outweigh the risks. This chapter outlines some of the key risks, allowing you to move forward with both eyes open. Of course, there is no safer or better way of assessing the risk than through a confidential conversation with experienced *qui tam* counsel.

Your Name Will Be Made Known

One of the most significant risks you face is that your name will eventually be made known. Unlike an anonymous tip, to claim a reward under the DOJ whistleblower program, your attorney must file a lawsuit on behalf of the United States. Your name goes into the caption, which reads something like this: *United States, ex rel. [Your Name], Plaintiffs, versus [Company Name], Defendant.*

Initially, the complaint will be sealed. During that period both your name and that of the defendant will kept from the public. At some point, however, DOJ will ask the court to unseal the complaint. Once unsealed, the whole world can access the case. If DOJ intervenes, it will serve a copy of the complaint upon the defendant with the same caption.

The government has a policy against keeping cases permanently under seal. Therefore, even if the government declines and you drop the case, it is likely that the defendant will be able to get a copy of what you filed.

The effect may extend beyond your current employer. Although times are changing, being labeled a whistleblower can negatively affect your reputation in some industries. Some companies may not want to hire someone who has filed a lawsuit against their employer. Therefore, you'll definitely want to think through this risk and hire seasoned *qui tam* counsel to advise you before filing a complaint.

Time and Energy

Another risk is that filing a lawsuit will require much of your time, energy, and emotional investment.

Before filing, you must ferret out the facts and help your attorney put together a convincing case showing that there was fraud and that it resulted in a significant loss to the federal government. You'll also be called upon to help with issues at various times throughout the entire time a case is ongoing. It can add up to many hours.

Although it is hard to quantify, the emotional stress that goes along with being a party to a lawsuit is incredible. It's constantly on your mind. Even before the case is made public, you will have an emotional ride. For instance, because *qui tam* cases must be filed under seal, you cannot talk to anyone about it until the seal is lifted, perhaps two years later. The need to stay silent about something so important to you can result in discouraging feelings of loneliness and isolation.

After a case is unsealed, you will be able to discuss the case, but your energy and emotions will be further taxed. You may worry about what others think about you. You may face new challenges at work or home. If you are working for the company being sued, you may find that they ask your co-workers to find fault with your work performance.

The legal requirements can be wearing as well. It is never fun to have your deposition taken. If the case does not settle before or at the time that DOJ intervenes, the lawyers for the defendant will certainly take your deposition. You may be asked questions under oath for an entire day. Although you will be accompanied by your attorney and given reasonable breaks, it won't be a pleasant experience.

Retaliation

The whistleblower law has a special provision that permits special damages to an employee who was "discharged, demoted, suspended, threatened, harassed or discriminated" because of assisting in a whistleblower case or investigating whether to bring a fraud case. The False Claims Act permits not only reinstatement, but permits *two times* the amount of back pay, plus other costs, and attorneys fees. Of course, to rely upon the remedies in these statutes, you would have to file a suit to be reinstated and collect these penalties.

There is a good reason why Congress needed to include this type of a provision: it is not unusual for wrongdoers to consider retaliation against whistleblowers. The fact that there is a rule requiring double damages may not be enough to prevent retaliation. It is possible to lose a job or be passed over for promotion, regardless of pointing out to your employer that you think their conduct has violated the whistleblower law.

Even if the treatment does not amount to retaliation, you may find it uncomfortable to stay at your job. You could be ostracized or given mundane work. The loss of employment is a real issue to consider before filing a *qui tam*. It is also possible that a defendant would file a slander lawsuit against a whistleblower. Although truth is a defense to slander and libel, it can be upsetting and costly to litigate.

Risk of Paying Attorney Fees and Costs

As discussed earlier, the whistleblower law provides that, if the government declines to intervene and the whistleblower still proceeds with the case, the court may award the defendant reasonable attorneys fees and expenses, if the defendant wins the case and your claim was "clearly frivolous, clearly vexatious, or brought primarily for the purposes of harassment." Again, this does not mean simply losing the case, but acting with improper motives. In addition, this risk can be totally avoided if the whistleblower agrees to drop the case if DOJ does not take it over. That is the safest course of action. It is followed 80 percent of the time by whistleblowers.

The Odds are Against You

Based upon statistics, the odds are against you receiving a reward in a declined case. Less than 25 percent of the time does DOJ take over a case. Even with the help of an experienced *qui tam* attorney, there is no guarantee that DOJ will intervene.

While your likelihood of a reward goes up dramatically if DOJ intervenes, the amount of a reward might not be as high as you hope. Although the average reward amount is reported to be $1.75 million, other statistics paint a different picture.

The reason the average amount is so high is that there have been several rewards of $100 million. For every $100 million jackpot, there are some under $100,000. Otherwise the average would not be $1.75 million. Actually, the "mean" or "median" reward amount is probably closer to $250,000. You will also need to pay your attorney and taxes out of the reward amount.

The point is that you cannot judge your case based upon statistics. And your decision to file should not be based solely upon whether you might get $250,000 versus $2 million. The new breed of whistleblowers desire to see the right thing done. They accept the patience and resolve needed to team up with DOJ in seeing justice prevail.

What you need most at this point is not more statistics, but the honest appraisal from an experienced *qui tam* attorney. Ask your attorney to evaluate the risks based upon your facts and to provide you with the reasons for his estimates of whether DOJ may intervene and what the case might be worth.

Money Doesn't Buy Happiness

Many people play the lottery hoping to cash in so they can kiss their jobs goodbye. They dream of a blissful life the winnings are supposed to provide. You may have similar goals in mind when deciding whether to file a *qui tam*. However, as the old saying goes, "Money doesn't buy happiness." If you were to interview everyone who received a million dollar reward or won a lottery, very few would say they are truly happier today.

Reporting fraud may be the right thing to do, but that does not mean becoming rich will bring peace to your life. There are simply greater things in life than wealth; such as family, country, and God. In short, there is a high cost to be paid — certainly emotionally and perhaps financially — for blowing the whistle. Also, if you treat the case as a lottery ticket, you won't invest the time and energy needed to win.

Perhaps the best reason to report fraud is not to obtain a reward, but to satisfy a feeling inside that shouts, "I cannot just look the other way." Following your conviction is the best medicine for enduring the risks associated with standing up and reporting fraud.

In summary, weigh your decision carefully. Seek solid legal and practical advice from your attorney. In the end, however, the decision must be your own.

CHAPTER TWENTY

A Checklist to Follow

Leave nothing for tomorrow which can be done today.

— Abraham Lincoln

The Checklist

From what you've read so far, you now know that the amount of fraud committed against the federal government is staggering. DOJ not only wants your help fighting fraud, but it is willing to pay significant rewards, if you bring the right kind of a case.

The following mini-checklists can assist you in making the important decision whether filing an application may be right for you. Keep in mind that these checklists should not be taken as legal advice. They are not a substitute for a consultation with an experienced attorney, who can review your particular facts and circumstances. Nonetheless, they will give you an overview of the kinds of things you'll need to think about, when you consider filing a case. The next chapter will help you piece this information together through a detailed questionnaire and prepare you for contacting counsel.

Step One: Evaluate Your Case

The first step is to evaluate whether you have the right kind of case for DOJ's whistleblower program. After reading through the types of cases illustrated in this book that historically produced actionable fraud, your preliminary evaluation should begin with a critical evaluation of the *Four F Factors*. You may not be able to adequately analyze these factors without the benefit of counsel, but it is useful to know what the considerations must be.

Filing first
Format is fundamentally correct
Fraud under a federal program
Funds are forfeited

Filing first gives you an imperative. Because only one whistleblower can receive a reward, you should not delay in contacting counsel. Your counsel can then evaluate your claims and discern whether or not anyone has already filed on the same issues.

With respect to the second *F Factor* (meeting the procedural aspects of the statute), your best approach is to hire experienced *qui tam* counsel.

Under the third *F Factor*, you must give careful scrutiny to whether the government lost significant funds under a federal contract or program as a result of the fraud you are alleging. The conduct must have been knowingly false, not an honest mistake or a poor buying decision. In addition, DOJ must be able to either convince the defendant to settle the claim or a court to order repayment that the payment requests were false.

The final *F Factor* includes the ability of the wrongdoer to repay the funds. Therefore, whether the company is in bankruptcy is something to weigh. If DOJ cannot collect much money, your reward may be too small to warrant the effort.

Checklist One
Am I the first to file a *qui tam*?
    Yes ☐   No ☐   Not sure ☐

Will my attorney strictly follow the process?
    Yes ☐   No ☐   Not sure ☐

Did the target deliberately commit fraud under a federal program?
    Yes ☐   No ☐   Not sure ☐

Can the target repay the funds?

Yes ☐   No ☐   Not sure ☐

Evaluation of Checklist

If you answer no to any of these, you probably do not have a good case and might want to keep your eyes open for another opportunity instead. If you are not sure on some answers, it does not mean that you don't have a case worth pursuing. Rather, you will need to be upfront with your attorney on these points.

For instance, it is hard to disprove that someone else filed first, so an uncertain answer there is not significant. To aid you in this point, however, I have attached as an appendix helpful ways how to conduct some basic research to find out if the same allegations are already being pursued. (See Appendix, *Conducting your own research*.)

You should be prepared to articulate why you think the target committed "fraud" and that federal funds or property were wrongfully paid out as a result.

It is also difficult to assess whether a target can or will repay the funds. While it is impossible to say whether or not a company will attempt to file for bankruptcy if they lose the case, it is possible to discern whether they are currently in bankruptcy proceedings and whether they currently have the capacity to pay. A certain element of the unknown will exist when the DOJ attorneys complete their analysis as well. The best solution is to gather the facts and have a qualified attorney make an informed guess.

Step Two: Consider the Prohibitions

The second step is to judge whether one of the three primary statutory prohibitions apply. If there are prohibitions, you may not have a valid claim.

One notable prohibition is that you cannot use the DOJ program to simply allege income tax evasion. Of course, the IRS now has its own version of the reward program, which is discussed in Section Three.

Next, if all of the fraudulent funds were paid out more than ten years ago, and in some instances six years, the case may be prohibited. You will need to ask your attorney to evaluate this issue and determine whether the six- or ten-year rule applies.

Third, if the allegations were the subject of a public disclosure — such as a newspaper article or published government report — the case may be prohibited. You may need to show that you fit the requirements of an "original source." You definitely will need the help of an experienced *qui tam* attorney to assess the public disclosure bar and original source exception issues.

Checklist Two
Was the fraud tax evasion?

Yes ☐   No ☐   Not sure ☐

Are payments older than six years?

Yes ☐   No ☐   Not sure ☐

Was the fraud publicly disclosed?

Yes ☐   No ☐   Not sure ☐

If so, am I an original source?

Yes ☐   No ☐   Not sure ☐

Evaluation of Checklist
If you checked yes to tax evasion, you cannot file a *qui tam*. Rather, you need to file an application under the IRS Reward Program. (See Section Three.)

If you checked yes to the question regarding payments being older than six years, you still have a decent opportunity to prevail, provided some of the claims are less than ten years old. Generally the government can still proceed — if it files a lawsuit within three years of when a responsible government official reasonably should have discovered the fraud.

The date you file the *qui tam* actually stops the clock for DOJ. All DOJ must show is that certain ranking officials did not know of the fraud within the three years following the date you filed the application. DOJ routinely relies upon this ten-year extended statute of limitations. Therefore, you may still proceed to contact counsel if significant funds were paid out less than ten years ago. Be sure, however, to discuss this issue with your attorney so that he can quickly evaluate this limitation provision and save everyone the time and expense if the ten-year provision cannot be invoked.

If you checked yes to the public disclosure question, you will need to have a frank discussion with your attorney. He will need to evaluate the law and need to determine whether you can fall within the original source exception.

If, for example, you know for sure that there was a newspaper article that would lead a reasonable reader to conclude that the company committed fraud and you did not have direct or independent (firsthand) knowledge of the facts, you may not find the case worth pursuing. Yet, if you believe that DOJ is not aware of the case and that significant loss to the government resulted, you can still contact an experienced *qui tam* attorney to get his views. Many whistleblowers have been able to show that they are original sources of the information, even after some form of public disclosure has occurred.

Step Three: Be Sure You Have a Great Case

While thinking through your potential case, bear in mind the three types of disfavored cases. They were cases where:
1. the recovery amount will be small
2. the government knowingly consented in the conduct
3. there is an inability to prove that the defendant knew its actions were wrong.

With respect to dollar size, you probably won't find it rewarding to bring a case that is under a $250,000 loss to the government, which may yield a $50,000 pre-tax, pre-attorney share reward. Consider setting even a higher threshold value, such as $1 million as your benchmark. That way, you may receive somewhere in the range of a $200,000 pre-tax, pre-attorney share reward. An experienced *qui tam* attorney can help you evaluate the scope and size of the case before committing to filing a case.

After talking to counsel, you should balance the potential rewards by all of the known risks. Of course, it may not be possible for you to judge the scope of the fraud or dollar impact. That is why you need to hire counsel knowledgeable about the federal program at issue. They can make an informed judgment as to the extent of damages.

As far as proving that the defendant knew the actions were false or fraudulent, state why you believe individuals knew that their requests for payment were based upon false statements. Did the company cheat? If not, you may need to move on. If so, can you or DOJ prove it? These are important steps. It may mean that you need to gather more facts.

On a more subjective level, if the case does not have any jury appeal (*i.e.*, there may have been a technical violation, but it was not material), DOJ may steer clear. For instance, if a doctor was required to follow ten steps in performing a minor procedure, but had a nurse complete one of the more routine steps, and the procedure was successful, one could argue that there was a violation of the Medicare regulations. However, it is clear that the procedure was covered by Medicare and the proper amount paid. No jury would be expected to require the doctor to refund the entire amount for some technical issue. The point is that DOJ can be expected to view the allegations from the perspective of a judge or jury, and not just the letter of the law. In addition, it is possible that a government official consented to the one step being performed by a nurse. It is common for healthcare providers to seek guidance from Medicare, and that can kill the appeal of a fraud claim.

Checklist Three
Is there a significant dollar loss?

Yes ☐   No ☐   Not sure ☐

Did the government know of and approve the conduct?

Yes ☐   No ☐   Not sure ☐

Can you prove guilty knowledge?

Yes ☐   No ☐   Not sure ☐

Is it a mere technical violation?

Yes ☐   No ☐   Not sure ☐

Evaluation of Checklist
If there is not a significant dollar loss, DOJ cannot be expected to spend two years investigating the allegations and even more time

proving it. If you know the scheme was widespread and likely resulted in a significant loss of dollars, you do not have to know the exact dollar amount. But if, for example, you only know of one instance of false claims and have no real evidence that it was extensive, you may not make the top of DOJ's priority list. Perhaps your *qui tam* attorney has enough experience to develop the case needed to convince DOJ to investigate and take over the case. Therefore, you may still want to contact counsel. Just be upfront about what you know or suspect, and ask for help in what additional information needs to be gathered.

If the government knew of the alleged false claim or contract violation at the time, but was actively working with the target to provide an acceptable solution, the case will be a tough road. Similarly, if all you can show is that there may have been a mere technical violation that did not result in a significant loss to the government, you may join the majority of whistleblowers in the declined status.

A good case usually involves situations where the government can state that, if it had known the truth, it would not have paid the defendant for its contracted services. The best chance of receiving attention from DOJ attorneys are instances where you can show guilty knowledge, meaning that the company knew it was cheating. That is the crux of the whistleblower program and the mark of great case.

Step Four: Choose Your Attorney

Assuming your checklists indicate that you have a case that may meet the requirements and recover significant funds, the final step is selecting your *qui tam* attorney. This stage is very important. The efforts by your attorney in presenting your case to DOJ can be a big factor as to how the DOJ attorneys perceive your case. Again, you should choose a *qui tam* attorney based upon a combination of their legal ability and personal attributes.

As to ability, they must be able to properly evaluate your case, present a convincing application that meets all of the requirements of the statute, and work well with DOJ. Plan to ask them what prior *qui tam* and government contract experience they possess. Ask them if they take a cooperative or confrontational approach with DOJ.

With respect to personal qualities, this is a subjective determination made individually by each whistleblower. You want to hire an attorney that you are comfortable interacting with. After meeting them, do you have confidence that they will keep you informed and treat you with the appropriate concern and care? You will be connected to them for several years, so it is important to select someone that fits your personality. After you have made your selection, trust them. Although you can expect regular updates, don't be a pest. Reread this book to keep a proper perspective, and then be patient.

As far as finding an experienced *qui tam* attorney, visit my website (www.HowToReportFraud.com), which contains more information on selecting an attorney.

CHAPTER TWENTY-ONE
Piecing it all Together

You are ambitious, which, within reasonable bounds, does good rather than harm.

— Abraham Lincoln

You are now ahead of the game. You have sampled the general types of fraud cases in which large DOJ rewards have been paid. You have been exposed to some common pitfalls to avoid and some significant risks to consider. Most likely, you realize that there is much more to learn. In fact, when I asked a friend to read this book while it was still in draft form, here is what he said:

> There are times you almost scare the person away — perhaps you should tell them that they should contact you to evaluate their case. I tried to think about how I would proceed, if I were a potential applicant, answering your questions about the *Four F Factors*. The problem would be that I would have no idea what I really knew and what I might be able to dig up. I would feel so much better if you asked me a lot of questions and then helped me determine what else I need to find out to prove fraud.

He was right on target — even with respect to scaring people away. First, your attorney should provide a framework for you to answer questions rather than figure everything out. Second, this book was meant to bring an element of sober judgment. While it should not scare you away, it should highlight that it would defeat the purposes of the program for 10,000 people to file applications tomorrow based only upon a hunch. That would needlessly drain the limited DOJ resources. In the end, Congress might eliminate the program if it stops being effective.

Being a modern-day whistleblower is not for everyone. Filing for a DOJ reward is a lot of effort. That is why this book purposefully does not sugar coat the process. It is often better not to file an application than to regret doing so a year or more later.

Having said this, DOJ does want whistleblowers to step forward and report fraud. If you have concerns, your greatest protection is to hire qualified *qui tam* counsel. Remember, that what you tell him remains confidential. Then, after receiving advice and weighing the risks, you can make an informed decision whether or not to file.

While you can get a good start on evaluating the *Four F Factors* by yourself, you still need the advice and opinion of an experienced *qui tam* attorney. Don't feel badly if you are not sure how to answer one or more of the questions from the checklists in the prior chapter. It took me many long hours, evaluating hundreds of cases, before I reached this level of expertise. I have provided these checklist questions to let you know what the key considerations are, not because I expect you to be able to evaluate a fraud case on your own.

You should expect your attorney to know how to ask you the right questions and to gather additional information needed to perfect your application. In fact, this issue is so important that I have developed my own screening tools, including a questionnaire. It serves two purposes. It puts you at ease by asking the right questions. It also goes to the heart of the issue and positions your case to be properly evaluated. This questionnaire is longer than what many law firms may use, but my long years of experience at DOJ have taught me what information will really be needed.

Take the time to work through the questionnaire at the end of this chapter, and write out your answers. It will force you to be more articulate and detailed. It will also highlight any additional facts that may be needed. Frankly, if you are not willing to go through the effort of filing out a long form, you won't have the staying power needed to collect a DOJ reward.

Finally, it is better to find out early if you have a potentially good case than discover many months or years from now that you have wasted your time.

Crunch Time

Are you ready to have your case evaluated? Then start your homework. First, select a *qui tam* firm. Don't plan to shop one attorney after another. Start out with your first choice, the one you believe is the best fit in terms of experience with the reward program and good working relationship with DOJ. You may have other criteria, such as certain personal qualities important to you.

Second, contact them. If that firm decides not to take your case, there likely is a good reason. You might wish to ask a second firm about your case, but keep in mind that you don't simply want to find any attorney who will file a case in the outside hope that DOJ might pick it up. Remember, there are risks to weigh, and it is counterproductive in the fight against fraud to load down DOJ with marginal cases. The quality of your counsel will make a difference. If two or three reputable firms, specializing in *qui tam* cases, decline to take your case, it may be time to reconsider.

When writing out your answers, be guided by these three principles:

1. Be truthful, without exaggerating
2. If you are not sure about something, say so
3. Provide as much detail as possible.

For some of the more detailed questions about the scheme or evidence in support, plan to write several paragraphs.

Confidential Questionnaire

Federal and State Fraud Questionnaire (Other than Tax Fraud)

1. Name, address, email address, and telephone number
2. Are the allegations that someone cheated the "Federal" Government? (Yes or No)
3. Are the allegations that someone cheated one a "State" Government? (If yes, identify which State.)
4. Briefly explain the fraud allegations, without mentioning the names of either the person or company that committed the fraud.

5. Why do you believe it was fraudulent, rather than an innocent mistake by the company or a poor buying decision by the government?

6. How much money would you estimate the government either has wrongly paid or has been financially harmed by the fraud? (In your response, describe how you calculated or estimated the amount.)

7. How did you become aware of the fraud?

8. Do you have any documents to help prove the fraud? (If so, briefly state the type of documents.)

9. When did the fraud occur? (Please state which years, when it stopped, and if it still going on.)

10. Did you once work for the company committing the fraud? (Yes or No)

11. Do you now work for the company committing the fraud? (Yes or No)

12. Did you make any complaints about the fraud to the person or company that committed the fraud? (If yes, without mentioning any names, briefly state what you did and how they responded.)

13. At the time of the fraud, did anyone at the government know of the acts which you think were false or fraudulent? (If yes, without mentioning any names, briefly state what they knew and how they knew it.)

14. Have your allegations been previously disclosed — as the subject of any legal action, newspaper story, lawsuit, agency hearing, congressional hearing, or government audit? (If so, briefly describe them without mentioning any names.)

15. Have you talked to another attorney about this matter? (Yes or No)

16. Have you filed a lawsuit against anyone or a company before? (If yes, briefly describe them without mentioning names.)

When I ask a potential whistleblower to fill out a form like this, I instruct them not to include the name of the company or individuals engaged in fraud or give answers so specific that they could refer to only one company. To me, the primary purpose of this form is to allow me to initially gauge the nature, size, and strength of your potential case. This information will facilitate any future discussion we may have. It provides a good framework for discussion and initial evaluation.

Some attorneys refer to this type of form as an intake form. They also ask for the name of the defendant upfront. They use that information to check for any conflicts of interest, such as if they already are investigating that company before reading the rest of your information. Both approaches, asking for the name of the defendant or asking simply for an overview of the allegations, are equally acceptable as long as your attorney truly treats this form simply as a starting point. After they review your form, they will contact you for more details if they think you have a potential case or will inform you that your case does not likely fit their criteria.

When sending your responses to an attorney, expect to receive a qualification that they have not agreed to represent you, but will use the information to make a determination as to whether you have a potential case and whether they want to become your attorney. A typical disclaimer may look something like this:

> *Before sending us this information, be sure you agree with the following statements:*
>
> *Although we will treat the information confidential, the transmission of any information is not intended to create, and receipt does not constitute, an attorney-client relationship. Even if you submit the questionnaire to me, that does not make me your lawyer. Instead, we will use your information to investigate the matter and to determine whether we can and will represent you in bringing your whistleblower case. Only when we both sign a written agreement will we actually become your lawyer and advocate. A fraud case can take a number of years from start to finish and it can be expensive for a lawyer to take a case. Therefore, we conduct a thorough analysis of cases and we do not accept every case. It may take time to evaluate your questionnaire and we may be busy on other matters at the time you send your questionnaire. If our time constraints do not fit your needs, you may wish to discuss your matter with another attorney.*

Don't be shy about providing detailed information in these forms. Although providing information does not create an attorney-client relationship, as a matter of law the information is treated as confidential. This means that your attorney cannot share this information with others or use it for their own personal benefit.

In short, be upfront in your responses. Remember, the questionnaire serves many important functions. It sets a good starting place for your initial conversation with an attorney. It also facilitates the attorney's understanding of your case so that he can respond to questions that you may have. Finally, it positions them to ask good follow-up questions in order to decide whether to take the case and, if they do take it, how to develop a good investigative plan before filing the case. That is why I ask all of my potential clients to first fill out a form like this prior to talking to me about a potential case. It saves time and helps avoid any misunderstandings.

Of course, the questionnaire is just the first step, but it can be a giant leap, if done well. So, plan to devote sufficient time to filling in your answers.

What if I Receive a Rejection Letter from an Attorney after Filling out the Form?

A rejection letter does not necessarily mean that you do not have a valid case, but it should put you on notice that there may be some higher risks. For instance, if a case does not meet one of the *Four F Factors*, don't expect an attorney to invest his time or resources.

Sometimes the reasons attorneys turn down case is for reasons apart from the validity of a case. They simply may be too busy to take on a new case or the amount of the case is too small to justify the amount of time and resources it will require.

If your case is rejected by a veteran attorney for reasons other than dollar size, you need to be wary of forging ahead using an inexperienced attorney. This is perhaps the largest reason why DOJ rejects 75 percent of cases. Inexperienced attorneys are willing to throw marginal cases at DOJ and hope for the best. This is a source of frustration I had while working for DOJ. In fact, it hurts the reward programs by distracting the government attorneys from working on strong cases.

Never forget that the assigned government attorney is a human being. While they enjoy working on valid claims of fraud, they may hate wasting time on "dog" cases. Each government attorney is assigned multiple cases at a time. Therefore they must make assessments and decisions regarding how much time and resources to spend on each case.

While at DOJ, when I was assigned a new case, I often asked my government colleagues about their interactions with the counsel for the whistleblower. I wanted to know what to expect. Do they work cooperatively with the government? Do they file marginal cases? Are most of their cases rejected? The Civil Fraud Section of DOJ in Washington, D.C. keeps a database of all *qui tams* ever filed. It is searchable by a variety of ways, including by the names of legal counsel that have represented whistleblowers under the program. I frequently searched the database to see what cases the particular attorney representing the whistleblower had filed before, and how many times the government took over or rejected those cases. Reputations do matter.

Frequent questions asked of me now that I represent whistleblowers are: "What criteria do you use in selecting cases?" and "How can a potential whistleblower ask me to review their case?" You can find this information in the section at the back of this book entitled *About the Author*. You can also visit my website, www.HowToReportFraud.com.

CHAPTER TWENTY-TWO
Case Study Revisited

No legacy is so rich as honesty.

— WILLIAM SHAKESPEARE

Having become acquainted with the DOJ Reward Program, it is time to look again at the initial case study. You should be able to better appreciate the events now that you know some of the requirements and pitfalls.

As you'll recall, the case study began with a description of the whistleblower. Mr. Jamison was a mid-level employee with a medium income. Mr. Jamison knew that his company was cheating, and was willling to step forward. To DOJ, this modern-day whistleblower was a hero. It was not necessary for him to talk with a silver tongue or wear stylish clothes. He was willing and able to link with DOJ to put it on the trail of proving fraud.

One of the key elements that led to his success was that Mr. Jamison hired an experienced *qui tam* attorney. His attorney, Mr. Duncan, guided Mr. Jamison long before they set foot in the hallways of the DOJ. He listened to Mr. Jamison's story and helped him fill in the missing pieces. For instance, he encouraged Mr. Jamison to make a copy of smoking gun documents, and then helped Mr. Jamison understand the importance of the documents. Together they came up with a list of people who could corroborate the fraud and locations where DOJ could find other documents to prove the case.

Although the case study did not present the full extent of his role, Mr. Jamison's attorney was a model. He spent over 1,000 hours helping DOJ conduct legal research and reviewing dozens of boxes of documents. Mr. Duncan worked cooperatively and closely with DOJ. He was a team player and became, in effect, an extension of the arm of DOJ.

By giving DOJ a smoking gun document, a detailed written description of the fraud, and good reason to believe that there was significant loss to the government, Mr. Jamison captured DOJ's interest. It didn't take long for DOJ to decide to form a task force and dedicate resources to investigate the allegations.

After sharing all that he knew, Mr. Jamison braced himself for a waiting game. Of course, there were times when DOJ asked questions — such as who else might know of the fraud and where to look for documents — but Mr. Jamison was no longer the center of attention. His attorney helped him understand the long, often slow process of proving a case and reaching a settlement with the company.

Initially, the crucial decision for Mr. Jamison was whether to ask his lawyer to actually file a *qui tam* lawsuit, a prerequisite to receiving a DOJ reward. Mr. Jamison was told of the risks. He knew his name would be made known. He also knew that, in most instances, DOJ does not proceed. Although Mr. Jamison was not motivated solely by the money, it would be welcomed. But his overriding motivation was doing the right thing. He knew that the company was cheating in many of its contracts and that the loss was costing the government (and ultimately the tax payers) millions of dollars. As a man of principle, he could not keep silent.

It took DOJ a year to formally decide to take the case. Afterward, the company used the legal process of discovery to try to keep Mr. Jamison from receiving a reward.

Mr. Jamison's attorney took an active role throughout: first by protecting Mr. Jamison; second, by helping DOJ. In serving as Mr. Jamison's attorney, Mr. Duncan had to wear many hats. He needed to reassure Mr. Jamison on a personal level, but he also had to exhibit great legal skill in countering the motions of the top lawyers hired by FlyX. At the same time, he had to work as a team member with DOJ by filling in the gaps, reviewing documents, or researching legal points. All the while, Mr. Jamison's attorney needed to ensure that there were no missteps or overlooked requirements of an exacting DOJ reward statute. A single mistake could have rendered his client ineligible.

As indicated, DOJ conducted an investigation that lasted a full year before making the decision whether to intervene. Actually, the average time is closer to two years. Because DOJ corroborated the allegations and had evidence of intent and significant damages, it decided to take this case.

Once DOJ makes that type of a decision, it rarely is proved wrong. And this case was no exception. DOJ dedicated as many resources as required to gather and review company documents, conduct interviews, and take and defend dozens of depositions. DOJ assigned three staff attorneys and the agency assigned two auditors and two full-time investigators. It even used the help of other government investigators during the initial interview stage. Mr. Duncan also took many of the depositions. It was a great team effort.

Over the next year, the whistleblower and his attorney were put to the test. FlyX filed numerous motions and discovery requests that took time, energy, and resources. Mr. Jamison's lawyer needed to convince a judge that Mr. Jamison was entitled to be a whistleblower and share in the proceeds of the case.

The first motion filed by FlyX was to dismiss the entire case, arguing that there was no legal remedy available to DOJ and the allegations had not been not pled with sufficient particularity. Specifically, FlyX argued that, even assuming that the allegations were true, there were no actual damages and, therefore, the case could not proceed. This was a turning point in the case. If the defendant was correct, the judge would dismiss the case. The case hung in the balance of a legal interpretation of a statute. It required solid legal analysis.

The next set of the defendant's motions were directed to Mr. Jamison. The goal of the company was to prevent Mr. Jamison from sharing any of the proceeds. It argued that Mr. Jamison really did not know much, if anything in particular, about the fraud. It pointed out that Mr. Jamison had not participated in the alleged activities and had not attended meetings where the purported fraud was discussed. The only evidence he had was a single document that suggested fraud.

The company drafted written questions and document requests in hopes of soliciting admissions that Mr. Jamison was not an original source of the knowledge of the fraud, then Mr. Jamison underwent a seven-hour deposition conducted by FlyX's lawyers. Because his lawyer was seasoned with *qui tam* experience, he was able to keep a level playing field between Mr. Jamison and the defendant.

The real test was whether Mr. Jamison would be governed by the original source rule and, if so, could he meet it. There was an issue regarding the amount of information Mr. Jamison possessed. FlyX argued that it was not sufficient to overcome the public disclosure bar. Under that rule, if a public disclosure exists, the whistleblower must have direct and independent knowledge of the fraud and have voluntarily provided it to DOJ prior to filing the *qui tam*.

Although it took the court a year to actually rule on the motion, it turned out to be a red herring. The need to prove "original source" status only applied if there had been a prior public disclosure of the allegations. Here, Mr. Jamison filed his *qui tam* suit before there were any media reports or other matters constituting a public disclosure. In short, the rule was not triggered. Therefore, the court did not examine if he was an original source. The defendant had tried mixing up and combining two rules that did not apply. The tactic was transparent to Mr. Duncan, as an experienced *qui tam* attorney. The only real danger to Mr. Jamison would have be if he had hired inexperienced counsel, who would not be able to recognize and defeat the clever, but unfounded, arguments of sophisticated lawyers.

Furthermore, Mr. Jamison's lawyer had already anticipated this maneuver and had taken steps to position his client to meeting the original source exception, should it have been found to apply. First, he had presented the information to DOJ in a meeting prior to actually filing the *qui tam* suit. Second, he helped his client gather additional information and copy internal documents that supported the fraud allegation. With this kind of legal experience on Mr. Jamison's side, a court would have been hard-pressed to rule against him, even under the direct and independent knowledge test.

Next, there was the issue of settlement. Here, DOJ accepted $70 million, where it might have recovered up to $210 million. While it might have been tempting to argue with DOJ and try to force it to hold out for the maximum $210 award available at trial some five years later, there was little assurance that there would be any assets to draw from, since the company was in bankruptcy. At its peak, the defense lawyers were likely charging the company $1 million a month to litigate. Other creditors had their feet at the door. Therefore, Mr. Jamison received wise counsel from his attorney that it was better to accept a certain $70 million, rather than seek to challenge in court DOJ's settlement position in the slight hopes of receiving more.

Finally, there remained the issue of what amount of a DOJ reward would Mr. Jamison receive. As indicated earlier, the reward can only be paid out of the proceeds actually collected from the wrongdoer. Here, DOJ recovered $70 million. How much of that amount would it pay Mr. Jamison? DOJ agreed to pay the whistleblower nearly 19 percent or $13 million. Although Mr. Jamison would have to share $5.2 million with his attorney, Mr. Jamison was still left with $7.8 million before taxes.

The 19 percent was determined by several factors. First and foremost, Mr. Jamison had not had detailed knowledge of the fraud. He did have a smoking gun and did cause an investigation, but he had only had documents relating to one of a dozen contracts. The timing of the settlement and large amount were also factors. However, DOJ wanted to give more than the minimum 15 percent because his attorney had been a valuable team player and the initial document had been so critical in the decision to open a full-scale investigation.

Other Rainbows

There are many other stories like this one that could be told, each filled with pots of gold at the end of their rainbows. But each happy ending shares at least two elements in common. First, the whistle-blowers hired quality counsel working as a team with DOJ. Second, the allegations meet the all-important *Four F Factors*.

Final Remarks Regarding the DOJ Reward Program

The first section of this book is designed to keep you from chasing after a mirage in a desert. There is a reason DOJ declines most cases. What you need is trustworthy advice, not empty promises.

Don't plan to file a *qui tam* on the off chance that DOJ may open a case and find something. You are unlikely to succeed and the distraction will actually hinder the efforts of DOJ in combating fraud.

Because it can take two years for DOJ to intervene in a case and additional time before a reward is paid, you will want to carefully decide whether the potential rewards truly outweigh the risks. You and your attorney need to be sure that you have strong evidence that the defendant knew its activity was fraudulent and that significant federal funds were wrongfully paid.

Remember, the DOJ Reward Program does not address waste or every poor buying decision by the government. In addition, not every reward will meet or exceed the national average. Moreover, keep in mind that there will be a lot of stress added to your life once you file a *qui tam* lawsuit. Obtaining a reward is like training for a marathon. You need staying power and a good coach.

The next two sections discuss the state reward programs and the new IRS Reward Program. Because both are based upon the DOJ Reward Program, you will be able to take what you have learned and apply it to those areas.

SECTION TWO:

The State Reward Programs

CHAPTER TWENTY-THREE

Rewards for Reporting State Fraud

Injustice anywhere is a threat to justice everywhere.

— MARTIN LUTHER KING, JR. (1929–1968)
(LETTER FROM BIRMINGHAM JAIL, APRIL 16, 1963)

Reporting fraud against the federal government is not the only source of significant monetary rewards. Many states have passed *qui tam* laws, modeled largely after the Department of Justice statute. The state reward programs work largely the same as the federal DOJ Reward Program, with one logical difference. They apply when there is fraud against the state, as opposed to the federal government.

The state reward statute is a perfect supplement to the federal *qui tam* statute, because there are many instances where the loss to the government is solely state funds. They also are a perfect partner because many state programs are partially funded by federal funds. Thus, if a state has a *qui tam* statute, the full amount of the funds can be recovered by a combined effort of the state and federal governments.

The DOJ Reward Program has proven so successful that Congress recently passed a law offering the states monetary incentives to adopt their own version of the DOJ Reward Program and the federal False Claims Act. One of the primary reasons is because fraud under the Medicaid program is a joint loss, affecting both the federal government and the states.

Congress is wisely interested in the overall health of each of its joint federal and state programs and wants to enlist private citizens to report such fraud. The best tool to stamp out fraud in these situations is to offer citizens rewards of up to 30 percent of the total recovery, just like under the DOJ Reward Program. In short, Congress wants to maximize the available rewards to whistleblowers to encourage as many as possible to join in the fight and pursue the full extent of the fraud.

Presently, 20 states have adopted reward statutes virtually mirroring the federal *qui tam* statute. They include: California, Delaware, District of Columbia, Florida, Georgia, Hawaii, Illinois, Indiana, Louisiana, Massachusetts, Michigan, Montana, New Hampshire, New Mexico, New York, Nevada, Oklahoma, Tennessee, Texas, and Virginia. Of these, three currently have limited the scope to health care fraud, which are Louisiana, Tennessee, and Texas. A few states are also starting to adopt tax fraud reward programs, such as Nevada.

Because the federal government has created a monetary incentive for all states to enact similar statutes, many more states currently are in the process of adopting similar reward statutes. Most states are expected to join this constant growing list. Information regarding state *qui tam* programs will be updated on my website (www.HowToReportFraud.com).

State False Claims Act Requirements

Nearly universally, the same technical requirements for the federal False Claims Act or DOJ Reward Program discussed in the previous chapters apply to state reward programs. In fact, the states adopt almost a verbatim statute as the federal law enforced by DOJ. Because of the similarities, courts often look to the federal program for guidance in deciding how to interpret the state laws. In other words, the amount of potential rewards available to citizens is the same in the state program as under the federal program. So too are the potential risks.

In short, the decisions facing a whistleblower as to whether to report fraud and apply for a reward are the same for state fraud as for federal fraud. Therefore, the section addressing the DOJ Reward Program is a useful guide for obtaining rewards under state reward programs.

Sample State Fraud Cases

In the short time that the state reward programs have been in effect, there have already been some large cases with significant rewards paid. These cases have recovered hundreds of millions of dollars. The following examples are based upon real state law cases and the amount actually recovered.

$187 Million. A bank chain improperly kept proceeds from unclaimed municipal bonds. (Note: These are funds that rightfully belonged to the state of California. However, the bank hid this information from the state in order to keep the funds. The whistleblower received a large reward for reporting this fraud.)

$40 Million. A company overcharged a state government relating to installment and monitoring of heating and cooling systems in state buildings.

$30 Million. A computer company sold defective computers to the state.

$30 Million. A construction company cheated during the construction of the Los Angeles subway system.

$14 Million. A hospital falsely reported the amount of its charity work and engaged in kickbacks.

$4 Million. A drug company was found liable for selling to nursing homes "repackaged" drugs that had been returned but not used and repaid millions of dollars from those sales.

There are also numerous state claims for Medicare and Medicaid fraud which have resulted in hundreds of millions of dollars in rewards. When state reward programs overlap with federal programs, larger rewards are paid to whistleblowers. In fact, tens of millions of dollars in rewards have been paid to whistleblowers under joint programs each year.

If you did not see a particular example of state fraud in the short list above, do not assume that means a reward was not available. In an effort not to be repetitive, I did not include types of fraud already mentioned in chapters about the federal program, but the same types of fraud are being committed against states as against the federal government. Rewards are given in either case or both.

In short, you can use this entire book as a tool for discovering fraud and applying for a government reward, whether the fraud is against the federal, state, or a combination of the two. In fact, the cases where state and federal losses overlap are likely to reap the greatest rewards for whistleblowers.

Do I have a State Fraud Case?

Since the state program is the mirror image of the federal DOJ program, this section of the book is intentionally short.

All of the chapters in Section One are relevant to answering your questions regarding whether you have a state case. For instance, you need to understand the *Four F Factors* of eligibility. These principles apply equally to state funds and federal funds.

The application process for the state program is virtually the same as that discussed in Chapters Eleven and Twelve, with the principle exception that your attorney will serve the state Attorney General instead of DOJ. The chapters discussing the government investigations and reasons why a case is declined also mirror the state program, as do the ranges and levels of rewards. The risks are also virtually the same. Even the checklist and questionnaire should be followed from the prior chapters relating to the DOJ Reward Program.

Here are a few important things to consider regarding state fraud reward programs.

First, even if you know of fraud against a state, that state must have passed a reward statute for you to be eligible for a reward. Presently, a dozen states have adopted such laws. Because this list of states keeps growing, you should check my website for updates regarding state law programs and which states are added to the list. (See www. HowToReportFraud.com.)

Second, it is possible that there was a joint effort with the federal government or a federal grant to the state. Therefore, the federal reward program might apply, even if you are in one of the states which have not yet enacted a reward statute. An experienced attorney can help decide this issue prior to actually filing an application.

Third, the next section, addressing the IRS Reward Program, contains a case study that includes a mixture of income tax fraud and state government fraud, which will aid in your understanding of the state program.

Finally, as with federal cases, be sure to carefully weigh the risks and select a competent attorney who has successfully handled many *qui tam* cases before. There are no second chances and there are many mistakes that cannot be effectively undone.

How to find a lawyer?

The same private attorneys handling whistleblower cases under the federal reward program also represent whistleblowers under state *qui tam* reward statutes. In fact, just as the courts look to the experience of the federal program in this growing area of the law, your best bet, when selecting counsel, is to rely upon an attorney experienced with the DOJ Reward Program. Thus, rather than repeat the process for selecting an attorney in this chapter, you are referred to the chapters in this book relating to selecting counsel under the federal program. You can also refer to the author's website for updated information, at www.HowToReportFraud.com.

Joint State and Federal Task Forces

Because the same types of fraud schemes occurring at the state level are also being committed against the federal government, the state Attorney General's Office coordinates its investigations with the Attorney General of the United States through the Civil Fraud Section of DOJ. While at DOJ, I worked together with many state Attorney General's Offices and combined our resources and investigative efforts.

The states also have a networking system between themselves to investigate overlapping fraud. Knowing how the states work with other government agencies is beneficial. In fact, it is often advantageous for a whistleblower's attorney to suggest investigative strategies to state officials which include other potential investigative resources.

As demonstrated in the case study addressing overlapping state fraud and tax evasion in the next section, a state might be more excited about taking a case where other agencies help share the workload.

Be sure to follow the checklists contained in Chapter Twenty and fill out the questionnaire from Chapter Twenty-One, only discussing your allegations of fraud against a state. This will position you to preliminarily evaluate your state claim and prepare you to contact counsel.

SECTION THREE:

The New Tax Evasion
Reward Program

CHAPTER TWENTY-FOUR

A Case Study: Tax Fraud Mixed with State Fraud

The income tax has made more liars
out of the American people than golf has.

— WILL ROGERS (1879–1935)

Are you ready to learn about the new IRS Tax Evasion Reward Program? As with the DOJ Reward Program, the best way to begin is with an example, which we refer to as a case study. This chapter outlines a case study of tax fraud mixed with some state fraud to bring perspective to this new IRS Reward Program. The following chapters will highlight its technical terms and keep your feet well grounded, so you can begin assessing whether you have a matter worth reporting. The following case study is an imaginary story designed to help you appreciate how a case develops. It also presumes that this book was an available resource relied upon by the characters.

Case Study: Seasons Greetings

Joanne was a rising college student with growing ambitions, hopes, and dreams. The high cost of her school tuition required her to work during the summers, weekends, and school breaks. During her three-week Christmas holiday, she put in exceptionally long hours working for the convention center in Washington, D.C.

The center was glad for the help during the rush of Christmas shopping. Each December, the jewelry industry hosted sales events where jewelry stores from across the nation would provide bargain prices on items from every woman's wish list — ranging from diamond jewelry, to gold and silver accessories. The prices typically were 40 percent lower than similar items sold at stores in the local malls. Needless to say, large crowds would visit the shows in hopes of gaining large bargains.

Joanne ran the cash register for the largest discounting company, *DiamondsR4Now*. The sales volume for a typical weekend show amounted to hundreds of thousands of dollars. The store manager would negotiate the prices with each customer using a series of internal factors and formulas, which were kept secret. Joanne would watch each negotiation and then, once a bargain was struck, ring up the sale. She was instructed, however, that if a sale was for cash, she was not to use the cash register, but to write up a receipt by hand. The boss liked cash sales, so he often told the customer that he would take an additional two percent off for cash and carry.

At the close of business the first day, Joanne asked why she was writing so many hand receipts. She observed that it slowed down the system.

The manager grinned and replied, "No records."

Joanne shrugged her shoulders, clueless as to what that meant. "Why does that matter?"

The manager said calmly, "No records means no sales tax or income tax."

Joanne was horrified to realize what this meant. Hundreds of thousands of dollars in income each week were not being reported because of her actions. The state was not getting its sales tax of eight percent on that money and the IRS was being cheated by numbers too high for her to fully grasp.

As the days wore on, Joanne could not clear from her mind the imagery of fraud being committed. She envisioned states cutting food programs for children due to lost revenues and other taxpayers being required to carry more of the weight. One night Joanne started jotting down numbers on a sheet of paper. She had a good idea of how many of the sales were cash and carry. Her eyes widened as the full weight of the fraud hit her.

According to her calculations, over the past six years, the company had failed to pay the various states a quarter of a million dollars in sales tax and the federal government millions of dollars in taxes. Joanne was aghast. The next day, she copied a few pages from the hand receipt book for evidence. However, she did not know what to do or whether anyone would really care.

Conscience Stricken

When Joanne returned to school the next week, her conscience was burning and she could not sleep. Therefore, she spoke to one of her professors. He gave her a copy of this book, *Whistleblowing: A Guide to Government Reward Programs*. He told her to read it carefully, because it not only discussed how to report fraud, but helped readers weigh the risks before stepping forward.

Joanne quickly discovered that her suspicions were right. This type of cheating was fraud against the government. She also learned that there were special offices designated to investigate fraud reported by a private citizen and, if she asked an attorney to file an application, she could receive a reward that would actually exceed her college debts.

Although rich rewards were a potential, Joanne was not driven by money as much as her concern about the unfairness of some companies not paying their share of taxes. The loss of revenues to the government affected how many programs could be offered to the truly needy. After a quick visit to the website noted in the book, she found out how to contact an experienced attorney to discuss her concerns. The attorney she contacted was experienced with the reward programs had worked with the author and knew exactly what to do. After reading the questionnaire she filled out, he agreed to represent her in filing for a reward.

Double Duty

Once he had reviewed the case, the attorney informed Joanne that *DiamondsR4Now* was actually cheating two separate government programs. Thus, the attorney filed for two separate reward applications on Joanne's behalf. The first was with the IRS for income tax fraud. The second was with several states that had similar programs for whistleblowers reporting fraud against state governments. The attorneys were able to take the receipts Joanne had kept and write up a compelling affidavit for Joanne to sign outlining the fraud scheme and statements by the owner of the store. They packaged the applications in a manner that would be enticing to overworked government workers in the IRS and Washington, D.C. local government leaders. They were pleased to seek recovery for the underpayments of sales tax, as well as income tax.

The Long Arm of the IRS

Joanne was glad to learn that the IRS was aware of these types of tax schemes, which are so common in weekend trade shows. However, the IRS often lacked the necessary probable cause to start investigations of specific companies without some inside help from citizens like Joanne. The IRS was grateful that her attorney had been able to provide a detail of the fraud scheme, estimate of damages, and other information regarding the way the company operated. It was sufficient to warrant an investigation against *DiamondsR4Now*.

The IRS seized the cash register receipts and handwritten sales receipts, as well as the books and records of the company. It did not take an auditor long to verify that the company was grossly under reporting income to the IRS. The IRS also provided its findings to the various states where the jewelry company had been avoiding state sales tax.

Together, the two agencies presented a formidable case against *DiamondsR4Now*. The company was willing to settle the allegations by turning over its entire bank account of $750,000 to the government. The owner of the store also pled guilty to a felony and was sentenced to 18 months in jail.

A Healthy Reward

Joanne was thrilled to know that her attorney had worked out a joint deal with the IRS and government attorneys for Washington, D.C. to pay a reward of 18 percent of the $750,000. Before taxes and attorney fees, she will recover $135,000 — far more than her college tuition. Joanne plans to use this money to pay for law school, so she can continue to make a difference in the world by protecting the rights of the disadvantaged.

CHAPTER TWENTY-FIVE

Requirements for IRS Rewards

*When there is an income tax, the just man will
pay more and the unjust less on the same amount of income.*

— PLATO (427–347 BC)

President Bush gave Americans an early Christmas present by signing into law on December 20, 2006 the new IRS Income Tax Fraud Reward Program. It is modeled after the DOJ Reward Program, but applies specifically to tax cheaters. While the wording of the IRS Reward Program is almost identical to the DOJ program for most substantive aspects, there are a few significant differences.

The IRS program is still in its infancy so it has not yet clearly defined all aspects of its new program. The IRS will undoubtedly periodically update its policies and procedures. Therefore, my website will provide current information, track changes, and identify any new procedures the IRS may adopt. (See www.HowToReportFraud.com.)

This chapter explores the history of the IRS Reward Program, the technical requirements, and the levels of rewards. The following chapters will provide you with a checklist and suggest a path to take in deciding whether and how to file for a reward. You will discover the basic requirements of the new law, learn how to prepare an effective application, and find out pitfalls to avoid.

History of the IRS Program

Congress had previously authorized the IRS to pay rewards to citizens when they stepped forward to report tax fraud. However, under the old rules, a citizen had few rights, the requirements were too exacting, and the decision process was so arbitrary that few meaningful rewards were actually paid.

For many reasons, there was a real need for an overhaul of the IRS Reward Program. In the past, only 1 out of 100 who tipped off the IRS received a reward. The majority of the time, the IRS did not even open an investigation. For those meeting the technical reporting requirements, just one in ten actually received a dime. Even then, the amounts of rewards were very small. Although there were a few years that the IRS paid rewards as high as seven percent, there were many more years in which the average reward was just two percent of the recovery. Rarely did the IRS pay out more than $500,000 in total rewards in any given year.

Needless to say, the IRS Reward Program was not much of a success. Fortunately, Senator Grassley, who championed the DOJ Reward Program, advanced a bill through Congress to revamp the sagging IRS program. It was modeled after the highly successful DOJ Reward Program, even using the same wording for the key features.

The New IRS Reward Program

Congress not only authorized the IRS to pay rewards in the range of 15 to 30 percent, it also required the IRS to establish a whistleblower office. To ensure that the program got off to a good start, it also commanded the IRS to report the progress of the program annually to Congress. No longer does the IRS have unfettered discretion to pay low awards. In most instances, the minimum reward must be 15 percent with a range as high as 30 percent.

The new program also dropped some of the strict requirements and a monetary cap. For instance, the old program denied a citizen the ability to use the help of an attorney by refusing to allow citizens to enter into contingency fee–type agreements which granted an attorney a share of the recovery. In effect, the IRS denied an applicant the use of legal counsel and advocacy. The old program also refused the applicant any rights of appeal. They had no bargaining power or say in whether or how much a reward should be paid. In addition, the old program set a cap or ceiling of $2 million for a reward.

Fortunately, the new program is warm and inviting. A whistle-blower now can rely upon an attorney to file the application and be their advocate, including negotiating the amount of a reward and contesting IRS decisions before the tax court. Gone also are the caps or limits in the amount to pay a whistleblower. Now, the whistleblower is entitled to a percentage of the total recovery, even if it amounts to $100 million.

In short, the whistleblower's attorney is involved in the process and may even appeal a low reward amount. This all adds up to a new face of the IRS that is using a carrot to entice citizens to report fraud rather than rely solely upon the big stick of the threat of a random audit against potential frauddoers.

Why is this program predicted to be so huge? The IRS collects $3 trillion a year. That is $3,000,000,000,000.00. The IRS has estimated that underpayment of taxes is between five and ten percent. Even assuming that the amount of fraud being committed each year is at the low end, the total fraud waiting to be reported is a staggering $150 billion. Congress has authorized the IRS to give up to 30 percent of this amount to whistleblowers, if proper claims are submitted. Thus, conceivably, the IRS could pay out more than $40 billion in rewards to citizens each year. How about that for a welcome change to the way you think of the IRS! And it would make good business sense for the IRS too. The IRS nets back 70 percent of funds it might never have known about. In other words, the more the IRS pays, the more it keeps. The IRS could gather tens of billions of dollars every year under this program.

Technical Requirements

The IRS Reward Program is fairly straightforward. It allows a whistleblower to receive a reward for reporting federal tax evasion. Although there may only be a few technical requirements for applying for an IRS reward, receiving a reward is another matter entirely. There are many strategic steps to follow if you want a realistic hope of actually receiving a reward.

One requirement is that the whistleblower must submit an affidavit stating that under penalty of perjury the information supporting the claim of tax evasion is true. The whistleblower must then either fill out a form or prepare a complete explanation of the tax fraud.

The paperwork requirement itself posses little burden, especially when a whistleblower enlists experienced counsel in preparing the application and presenting the information. Actually, this affidavit requirement is not designed to keep away good faith reports of tax evasion, but is rather an attempt to keep people from using this program as a weapon, simply out of spite, with no real goal of submitting a legitimate application. In other words, the IRS does not want to become embroiled in child custody disputes or other emotionally charged squabbles where the threat of reporting tax fraud is used as leverage. Requiring an affidavit helps reduce someone using this program on an impulse.

Unlike the DOJ program, the IRS Reward Program does not require that you use an attorney or actually file a civil complaint in court. (Although, there is good reason to enlist counsel.) As a result, the whistleblower cannot pursue the case if the IRS declines to open an investigation or closes the file without recovering any back taxes. Therefore, the initial application needs to stand out and a solid investigative plan built upon the evidence must be proposed. You can imagine that it is vital to put your best foot forward. I simply would not dream of simply submitting a standard IRS form to report fraud and expect the assigned agent to be excited about investigating my allegations. Rather, I treat the IRS program similar to the DOJ program it is modeled after and carefully craft a statement of material evidence in support of the allegations, including a proposed investigative plan for the IRS to follow.

Another distinction between the reward programs is that there is a minimum dollar threshold to be eligible for certain types of cases. Although there is no minimum amount of fraud needed for reporting fraud against a company, for pursuing tax fraud against "individuals" the person cheating must have had both, (1) a gross income of at least $200,000 during one of the tax years at issue, and (2) cheated by a total of $2 million.

Again, the IRS does not want to see its program used as a weapon in family or neighborhood squabbles. This requirement is designed to reduce that possibility. For instance, in a marital dispute, a divorced spouse might want to file a reward application alleging that her former spouse is cheating on taxes by claiming certain child expenses that might not be allowable. The motive may be more tied to anger or revenge that the IRS recovering $500 in improper tax deductions.

While it may be argued that the threshold of $2 million for individuals is overkill, that is the current threshold in the statute and it must be abided by. Actually, I personally set my sights on cases at this same threshold, and will not take a case under $2 million in unpaid taxes. (See the section, *About the Author*.) Your attorney will be in a better position to judge whether the fraud you want to report can meet the technical limits of the program. For instance, the IRS does allow you to combine the loss for each year and factor in interest and civil tax penalties that could be imposed. Your attorney can help you gauge whether you meet the requirement.

There is also an unexpected twist when computing the $2 million figure. This refers to the amount of unpaid taxes, not the amount of income not reported. For instance, if you reported that a person failed to report $2 million in cash sales, you would not meet this technical requirement. Assuming the person owes 30 percent in taxes, the amount of taxes owed on the $2 million in cash sales would be $600,000. To reach the $2 million threshold of unpaid taxes, the amount of unreported income would need to be close to $7 million.

Public Disclosure Bar

An additional point is that the IRS program adopted the same "public disclosure" bar as used in the DOJ program. In other words, if the IRS determines that there was a "public disclosure" as defined by the DOJ program and used here, then the amount of any reward is capped at ten percent, but could easily be zero. The IRS has wide discretion if it determines that the allegations were already in the public domain. Because this exception is word-for-word the same as the DOJ program, it is important to understand how DOJ applies this exception. You should refer back to Chapters Nine and Fifteen for a discussion of this public disclosure bar.

Protecting your interests in this area is something your attorney will need to be mindful of. He needs to be a strong advocate for arguing why this limitation does not apply. Because the program is so new, there are few existing court cases as precedents to support an attorney's interpretation of the IRS statute. Therefore, it is presumed that the same rules from the DOJ program will be applied in light of the language being identical. Once again, having counsel experienced with the DOJ program is your best bet.

CHAPTER TWENTY-SIX
Sample Tax Fraud

Income tax returns are the
most imaginative fiction being written today.

— HERMAN WOUK (1915–)

One of the more lucrative areas of tax evasion for you to report is improper shifting of profits offshore.

In a recent case, a large pharmaceutical company agreed to pay the IRS $2.3 billion for tax evasion after having shifted its profits offshore. The U.S. drug company had attempted to evade federal income taxes by transferring ownership of its drug patents to a company it formed in Bermuda. The entity in Bermuda was really just an empty shell of a company, with no real employees and no real work being performed there.

This company's scheme involved having the Bermuda branch of the company charge the U.S. branch of the company huge royalties for being allowed to sell drugs in the United States. The U.S. drug company claimed large deductions for these so-called royalties, thereby reducing the amount of taxes owed. Obviously, the expenses were fictitious. The Bermuda company did not perform any real services to justify the royalties. It existed only to create a royalty scheme that amounted to tax evasion. Because the companies were related entities, the IRS was able to pierce the corporate veil and consider the two companies as one.

If someone had properly reported this tax evasion scheme, they would have received $350 million or more as a reward! Although this scheme has already been uncovered, you can be sure that many other companies are engaged in this same tax evasion scheme today. This case is just the tip of the iceberg. Every day, huge companies are cheating the government of millions of dollars in taxes. This area is ripe for large rewards for those willing to ferret out the fraud and properly report it.

Today, many drug companies and high-tech companies are seeking to shift profits offshore. In addition to concealing ownership of patents, other schemes include transferring ownership of logos, manufacturing processes, and other intangible property rights to offshore companies, and then paying large fees to its offshore company. These schemes have increased in the last few years, and are waiting to be reported under the new IRS Reward Program paying up to 30 percent of the amount the IRS recovers.

Other Examples

The ways people and corporations cheat on income taxes is limited only by imagination. It does not matter what scheme is used, a reward is available for proving that there was an underpayment of taxes by any company and by individuals meeting a certain threshold amount. Below are other examples of tax evasion by not properly reporting income or by improperly claiming deductions:

- improper tax shelters
- putting assets in another person's name
- embezzling funds or committing securities fraud (and not claiming it as income)
- failing to keep or concealing records of income
- paying by cash to avoid any written record of income
- claiming deductions that are bogus
- lying about ownership of assets
- mischaracterizing capital gains
- failure to report capital gains
- hiding assets overseas

If a particular type of underpayment of tax is not listed, it does not mean that there is not a reward. There are simply too many types of tax schemes to attempt to create a comprehensive list. Under the new law, if a person had reported these fraud schemes, they would have received between 15 and 30 percent of the amounts recovered.

As with the other reward programs, you need to have solid evidence of underpayment and the amount must be significant. Your reward is entirely dependent upon convincing the IRS to not only open an investigation, but to recover the unpaid taxes.

CHAPTER TWENTY-SEVEN
Applying the "Four F Factors"

Truth is the only safe ground to stand on.

— ELIZABETH CADY STANTON (1815–1902)

As with any new program, the question is: "What Does It Take to Receive an IRS Reward?" The answer to that question is as simple as one word: documentation.

The IRS is not interested in hunches or speculation. If your neighbor owns five cars but works at McDonalds, don't expect the IRS to open a file. It is not enough to know in your heart that the person must be cheating on their tax returns. As might be expected, the IRS receives numerous reports of "cheating" from people trying to get back at one another for unrelated grudges or from those who think someone is cheating when they really don't have any idea if it's true or not.

An IRS reward is for those people who can *show* how another person is cheating by providing some concrete proof of underpayment of federal taxes. The most common method is by producing records that "document" the fraud. Perhaps it is a second set of books that you have copied several pages from or a collection of internal memos, letters, or emails that you have kept copies of, in order to prove tax fraud. The documents do not need to detail the whole fraud scheme, but should provide support to your allegation that the company or person has, in fact, underpaid taxes. (Again, you should not take with you documents prepared by company lawyers, which are privileged. Although you may need to check local rules, you are generally entitled to make copies of company business documents that are within your normal activities or duties.) Of course, if you have personal knowledge, but cannot obtain documents in support, the strength of your knowledge will be the key.

Let me make this clear. It is not necessary to take risks to get copies of documents. But you must be able to articulate just how the fraud is being committed. It also helps if you can describe what documents exist that the IRS can subpoena to prove the case. Remember, the IRS agents are interested in going after people cheating on taxes, but they don't want to spend years chasing after ghosts. They will pay you a reward, if you can put them on a solid trail of underpayment of taxes.

The final equation is the dollar amount of fraud. While cheating by $10,000 seems horrible to the average person, a busy IRS agent has hundreds of cases to investigate and only 40 hours in a normal work week. This actually raises the point of whether the more experienced law firms have an unspoken "minimum" amount of fraud by a company to take a case.

While the program does not set a minimum for reporting fraud against a company, realistically, you cannot expect the IRS to open an investigation for every allegation submitted. To attract a quality attorney to represent your interests, a rule of thumb might be $1 million in underpayment of taxes by a company.

In light of the fact that the IRS "minimum" for an individual is $2 million, many firms use that amount as a minimum for companies too. It would also not be surprising if one day the IRS imposes this limit if it starts getting too many applications from *pro se* individuals or those not well prepared, even with the help of inexperienced counsel.

As you contemplate the amount of underpayments, be mindful that the $2 million threshold is the amount of *underpayment* of taxes, not the amount of income not declared or bogus deductions claimed. To reach $2 million in repayment of taxes, the amount of underreported income or improper deduction may need to be $7 million (assuming a 30 percent tax rate). Again, your attorney will be able to include interest and tax penalties to reach the $2 million mark. In addition, the reward statute is triggered by the amount of underpayment, not the actual amount recovered. In the case study, the company had cheated by over $2 million, but the IRS was only able to recover $750,000. The whistleblower remained eligible, and received her share of the amount recovered.

Applying the Four F Factors

In Chapter Six, I coined the term *"The Four F Factors"* for the DOJ and state reward programs. These same four factors basically apply to the IRS program. Slightly modified to fit the IRS program, the *Four F Factors* are:

Filing First
Format is fundamentally correct
Federal taxes unpaid
Funds forfeited.

The IRS has not provided clear guidance on whether it will split rewards based upon level of information provided by a whistleblower or if it will follow the DOJ model of paying only one person, "the first to file." But for the time being, expect that only the first to file a proper application will receive a reward. In any event, you should not delay in contacting counsel and should not have loose lips in discussing your fraud allegations with others. (See Chapter Six.)

Next, the IRS Reward Program has a format requirement that must be followed.

This second factor requires that the whistleblower sign an affidavit under penalty of perjury that the information in the reward application is true to the best of their knowledge. Of course, if your submission stopped there, so would the hope of recovering a reward.

That was one of my frustrations as a government attorney. Some whistleblowers and inexperienced counsel were so focused on the technical requirement of what paperwork to submit that they often lost sight of preparing a compelling application. At DOJ, I declined four out of five applications, frequently due to improper preparation. What good it is to rush in an application that is so sloppy that it will be rejected?

The third factor is even more obvious. The program only applies to underpayment of federal taxes. The DOJ and state programs address fraud outside of taxes. Be mindful, however, of the threshold dollar limits already discussed.

The final factor is that the reward is paid from the amount of underpaid taxes which the IRS *recovers*. This means that, while the underpayment of taxes might be $3 million, if the IRS collects only $2 million, your reward is based upon the $2 million.

Statute of Limitations

There are two significant differences between the IRS Reward Program and the DOJ Reward Program worth discussing. First, the IRS Reward Program does not require proving any guilty knowledge. Second, the statute of limitations is drastically different between the two programs.

Under the DOJ Reward Program, the government must prove that the defendant knowingly submitted a false statement or claim for funds. By contrast, the IRS Reward Program does not require a showing of fraud or any type of intent. Rather, the whistleblower is rewarded with a portion of the unreported tax which the IRS recovers.

The statute of limitations, however, greatly affects the types of cases in which the IRS is likely to collect unpaid taxes. Under the DOJ Reward Program, there is a single statute of limitations for all types of cases, which is a minimum of six years and a maximum of ten years, depending upon when the government first learned of the fraud. Under the IRS Reward Program, there is no *per se* statute of limitations that applies to the whistleblower. Instead, there are general statute of limitations that affect the IRS from recovering taxes based upon classifications of unreported taxes. Of course, this has the practical effect of barring the whistleblower, as a reward is paid from the funds the IRS recovers.

Congress enacted a complex statute of limitations affecting the ability of the IRS to collect back taxes. It provides different time limits for different types of unpaid taxes. The general rule is that the IRS has three years to collect back taxes. There are, however, a series of exceptions. For instance, it the unreported tax obligation involves certain excise taxes or if the amount of unreported income exceeds 25 percent of the total reported income, then the statute of limitations is six years. There is another, more important exception, however. If a person or company files a fraudulent return or engages in a willful attempt to evade taxes, there is no statute of limitations at all. That means that theoretically you could file for a reward for tax fraud occurring 20 years ago.

Before you get too excited, you must convince the IRS to take such an old case. The IRS will be required to prove to the satisfaction of a court that the person or company knew that it was committing fraud. The court will demand that the IRS prove this guilty knowledge by clear and convincing evidence, which is a high burden. Normally, the burden in a civil case is the preponderance of evidence, which means that something is more likely than not. The clear and convincing standard approaches that of a criminal case which requires a showing of beyond a reasonable doubt. In addition, the IRS will face difficulty in proving the case because the evidence needed to prove fraud may be lost or destroyed.

Having said this, if you can convince the IRS that the person or company committed fraud and the IRS can prove it, you are eligible for a reward without regard to a statute of limitation. But remember, the IRS reward program does not allow a whistleblower to pursue a case in which the IRS declines. Thus, you must do everything in your power to get and maintain the interest of the IRS for a fraud case, regardless of its age. That is why it is so important to hire quality counsel and submit a compelling application. It won't be a technical requirement that prevents you from obtaining a reward so much as whether you can produce evidence that the person or company knew that they were cheating on their taxes and have the funds to pay the tax.

CHAPTER TWENTY-EIGHT

Risks and Rewards

> *Money never made a man happy yet, nor will it.*
> *The more a man has, the more he wants.*
> *Instead of filling a vacuum, it makes one.*
>
> — BEN FRANKLIN (1706–1790)

What Risks Do I Face?

In many ways, the risks in reporting tax fraud are similar to and different from the risks in reporting fraud under the DOJ Reward Program discussed in Chapter Nineteen. Below are highlights of some of the differences.

Confidentiality

Under the DOJ Reward Program, your name will be made known. The IRS, however, prides itself on maintaining confidentiality of its whistleblowers. It will not disclose your name to the tax cheater. However, this promise is not absolute and there is no guarantee that the tax cheater won't discovery your identity. In fact, there are some practical limitations on maintaining secrecy built into the IRS Reward Program.

First, the level of your reward is based upon your participation. The more you participate, the higher the award, but also the more likely the wrongdoer will figure it out. The tax cheater might guess that there was a whistleblower or that it was you by a process of elimination by talking to everyone in a position to know that they cheated.

Second, there may be some instances where the only way that the IRS can prove tax evasion is with your testimony. In other words, there may be instances where the only hope the IRS has of proving intent is if you testify that the tax dodger bragged that he was cheating. In those instances, either you testify or the IRS case disappears. If you don't allow your name to be used, there won't be any reward.

In most cases, however, the IRS will manage to keep your name confidential. But you need to know there are no guarantees that your name will never be made known.

Time and Energy

Just as with the DOJ Reward Program, it will take a lot of time and energy for you to earn a reward. It often takes years for the IRS to prove tax evasion and collect the money. You and your attorney will be asked to help the IRS understand and prove certain things along the way. Because your whistleblower reward can only be paid out of actual proceeds collected by the IRS from the wrongdoer, you may feel like you are caught up in a waiting game.

Other Important Issues

Don't delay. You should contact an attorney as soon as practical. The IRS reward program has a statute of limitations that is either three years for simple underpayment of taxes or six years for certain other types of underpayments, such as excise tax. In addition, even if there is no statute of limitations issue because you have a solid fraud case, if another person makes the case first, they may be the only one eligible for a reward.

Don't talk too much. Don't discuss your tax evasion allegations with anyone except your attorney. As discussed earlier, be prepared for the IRS to pay only one person for each case, the one who first submits a proper application. Don't risk someone else using your information to file a claim by talking too much about it to others.

Levels of Rewards

What amount of reward can you expect? As with the DOJ Reward Program, the IRS has set several ranges of rewards. The most common range is 15 to 30 percent. Essentially, the whistleblower receives a minimum of 15 percent with a sliding scale of up to 30 percent of the amount the IRS recovers. Again, this in not based upon the amount of unreported income, but the amount of tax due, and the actual reward is a portion of how much the IRS recovers. The exact percentage will be negotiated between your attorney and the IRS. The standard used to determine the exact percentage is:

> *The determination of the amount of such award by the whistleblower office shall depend upon the extent to which the individual substantially contributed to such action.*

In other words, the level of the reward is based upon a combination of how good your information was and how much effort you and your attorney contributed in assisting the IRS in recovering the funds.

In addition, the IRS has two reduced-fee categories. First, there is a reduced or eliminated reward if the whistleblower's application is based upon publicly disclosed information. This "public disclosure bar" is the same as the one used in the DOJ program, and applies when the application is:

> *based principally on disclosures of specific allegations ... resulting from a judicial or administrative hearing, from a governmental report, hearing, audit, or investigation, or from the news media.*

The most common way for this restriction to be triggered is when evidence of the fraud can be gleaned from reading the newspaper or Internet. In other words, if the IRS agents could figure it out themselves from watching the news or surfing the Net, there is no need to pay you a reward.

If the public disclosure bar applies, the IRS has discretion to "award such sums as it considers appropriate, but in no case more than 10 percent of the collected proceeds." Because of the discretion involved, your attorney needs to be a good advocate and knowledgeable of the intricacies of the public disclosure bar borrowed from the DOJ program.

There is one built-in exception to the public disclosure bar, namely, if the whistleblower is the one who caused the public disclosure in the first place. The bar also does not affect any applications filed before a news story appears in the media. In short, the IRS has a similar original source exception, like the DOJ program.

Because of the complex nature of this bar and the drastic affect on a reward, you will need to enlist an experienced attorney familiar with the DOJ Reward Program. They may be able to convince the IRS that the public disclosure does not apply in the first instance, and, even if it does, why the IRS should pay ten percent rather than zero.

The standard to determine the range of a reward in this situation requires:

> *taking into account the significance of the individual's information and the role of such individual and any legal representative of such individual in contributing to such action.*

Unlike the DOJ program, if the IRS declines to take your case, there is no opportunity for you to proceed to prove the fraud on your own. Recall that under the DOJ program, the attorney filed a civil lawsuit on behalf of DOJ and the statute allowed the whistleblower to continue with the case even if DOJ opted out. In those instances, the whistleblower would receive a higher amount, between 25 and 30 percent of the recovery. By contrast, under the IRS program, your entire reward depends upon convincing the IRS to take your case and recover funds. There is no appeal process if the IRS does not open an investigation or chooses not to require payment of back taxes. That is why it is vital that your attorney can be a good advocate in encouraging and assisting the IRS to take your case and vigorously pursue your allegations.

There are two bright spots to this truncated process of automatically terminating your case if the IRS does not proceed. First, there is no need for a provision allowing the tax cheater to seek any attorney fees against you if, in bad faith, you proceed with the action after the government declines. In other words, you are not liable to pay the defendant any attorney fees for defending against the allegations. Thus, there is one less risk in reporting IRS fraud than under the DOJ program.

Second, under the general provisions, the IRS allows higher rewards of between 15 and 30 percent rather than the DOJ range of 15 and 25 percent. That is an excellent tradeoff for not being allowed to proceed without the government because, in most declined DOJ cases, there is no recovery. Thus, the rewards for the IRS program may be even higher than the DOJ program. Recall that the average percent paid by DOJ was close to 18 percent. Because the IRS range is five percent higher, you can expect the IRS to pay average rewards of 20 percent or more in a typical case.

The final exception to the normal 15 to 30 percent range is the bar for those who "planned and initiated the actions that led to the underpayment of tax." This does not mean one who participated or carried out orders. But if you are the one who thought of the scheme or the one encouraging it to be carried out, don't expect a reward. However, those who are knowledgeable because they saw firsthand the fraud or even were asked to help carry out the scheme are being actively courted by the IRS and are likely to meet the definition of a whistleblower under the program.

Summary

Engaging an attorney familiar with the government reward programs is your best protection in reducing risk in reporting tax fraud. As far as whether, when, and how much of an IRS reward you may receive, it depends upon a lot of factors. It's hard to predict with any certainty. Be reminded, however, that you should not get so involved with trying to guess the amount that you forget about how strong a case you really have, and whether you or your attorney can effectively present it to the IRS.

CHAPTER TWENTY-NINE

The Application Process

If you tell the truth, you don't have to remember anything.

— MARK TWAIN (1835–1910)

This chapter provides you with a process for evaluating whether you may have a tax evasion case worth reporting. It includes a preliminary checklist for you to work through to test the case.

If you find that the case appears to have merit and your information may be valuable to the IRS, then you can move on to the detailed questionnaire that follows. It serves several purposes. First, it will determine if you are really serious about engaging in the process of applying for a reward. Second, it will provide you with the information an experienced attorney will need to evaluate your case and prepare a convincing application to the IRS officials. Third, after you have written out your answers, you will be able to see the details more clearly yourself. In any event, it will be time well spent.

The next chapter discusses whether you should file the application yourself (*pro se)* or use the services of an attorney. It is an important personal decision you will need to make. It lists some of the benefits to hiring an experienced attorney.

A Checklist to Follow

It is no secret that many companies and individuals are cheating on their taxes. The IRS wants to involve you, but only if you can present solid claim of an underpayment of taxes. Although not providing legal advice and not substituting for asking an experienced attorney to review your particular facts and circumstances, the following mini-checklists can assist you in making the important decision of whether to report tax fraud.

Step One: Find Out If You Meet the Requirements

Can you meet the statutory requirements using the *Four F Factors* criteria for tax evasion cases? As in a DOJ case, you may not know if you are the first to file, so the best approach is to contact counsel without delay.

With respect to the second factor, you must be willing to sign an affidavit stating under oath that the information is true. If you are serious about the case and have based your claim on solid evidence, this should not be a problem. Your attorney can draft the affidavit and review it with you before you sign it. Of course, you must also submit a compelling statement of the allegations. The affidavit merely states that the facts in the application are true.

Under the third factor, you must be able to show that significant funds were not reported in a tax return. This will be a deciding factor in whether the IRS opens a case and in determining how much of a reward you might receive. And if the claim is against an individual, the amount of underpayment must amount to a minimum of $2 million.

The fourth factor addresses the ability of the wrongdoer to repay the funds. If the company is in bankruptcy, it is a legitimate consideration. When the IRS cannot collect very much money, your reward may be too small to warrant the effort.

Checklist One

Am I the first to file?

Yes ☐   No ☐   Not sure ☐

Will I sign an affidavit?

Yes ☐   No ☐   Not sure ☐

Do I have proof of a tax underpayment?
                Yes ☐   No ☐   Not sure ☐

Are significant funds involved?
                Yes ☐   No ☐   Not sure ☐

For an individual, does it meet $2 million?
                Yes ☐   No ☐   Not sure ☐

Evaluation of Checklist

If you answer no to any of these, you may not have a good case and may want to keep your eyes open for another opportunity. If you were unsure of some answers, it does not mean that you don't have a case worth pursuing. Rather, you will need to be upfront with your attorney on these points. Of course, it is hard to disprove that someone else filed first, so an uncertain answer there is not significant. However, plan to conduct some research yourself, based upon the approach in the Appendix named *Conducting your own research*. In addition, the IRS may issue new policies soon that affect your evaluation of the checklist, so be sure to visit my website for any updates and changes to the program before giving up.

If you do plan to proceed, it is important that you are able to articulate why you think the person or company underpaid taxes, including the proof, as well as how you estimated the amount.

Step Two: Check Statutory Issues

The second step is to judge whether one of the statutory prohibitions apply. If they do, you may not have a valid claim. For instance, if the claims are too old, the IRS may not try to collect the funds or it may not be able to if the statute of limitations has expired. Next, if the allegations were the subject of a public disclosure, such as a newspaper article or published government report, you may need to show that you fit the requirements of an "original source." Of course, this may not act as a complete bar, like the DOJ Reward Program, so it may still be worth pursuing. You'll definitely need the help of an experienced *qui tam* attorney to assess the public disclosure bar issue and advancing your claim for why you meet an exception or should receive a higher percentage.

Checklist Two

Are underpayments older than three years?

           Yes ☐   No ☐   Not sure ☐

If so, can I show intent to defraud?

           Yes ☐   No ☐   Not sure ☐

Was the underpayment publicly disclosed?

           Yes ☐   No ☐   Not sure ☐

If so, am I an original source of knowledge?

           Yes ☐   No ☐   Not sure ☐

Evaluation of Checklist

The IRS program does not state that you must prove fraud to collect a reward, although it definitely will be more excited if you can prove fraud. The IRS Reward Program is broad enough to include mere underpayment of taxes. However, the statute of limitations for mistakes or general underpayment may be as short as three years. Whereas, there is no statute of limitations when you are able to show that they knew they were committing fraud. The IRS looks at a fraud case entirely differently. It can pursue any case where it can prove the company knew it was cheating, even if the underpayment was 20 years ago. Of course, there are the practical realities of proving an old case.

If you checked yes to the public disclosure question, you will need to have a frank discussion with your attorney. He will need to evaluate whether the public disclosure bar actually applies, which eliminates or greatly reduces the amount of the reward. Your attorney should also be able to make a determination whether you meet the original source exception to that bar, which would lift you back into the 15 to 30 percent range. For instance, if you know that there was a newspaper article that would lead a reasonable reader to conclude that the company underpaid taxes and you did not have direct or independent (firsthand) knowledge of the facts, you may or may not find the case worth pursuing. The bright spot is that you are not automatically excluded if there was a public disclosure and you don't meet the original source exception as applied by the DOJ Reward Program. However, the maximum range of reward is ten percent, with discretion to reward zero.

If you believe that the IRS is not aware of the case and that significant loss to the government resulted, you can still contact an experienced *qui tam* attorney to find out if you can meet the exception or if it remains worth reporting for a reward in the zero to ten percent range. Many whistleblowers have survived the public disclosure bar by being able to show that they are original sources of the information. A good attorney can be a strong advocate.

The other factor in your favor is that the defendant is not allowed an opportunity to raise this issue of the public disclosure bar or file a motion to exclude you from receiving a reward, as is permitted under the DOJ Reward Program. However, this does not make hiring experienced counsel any less important. Remember, you only get one shot at convincing the IRS as to your status. But once you do, you are nearly home free. The defendant is not allowed to second guess or become involved in the process. It is an issue between your attorney and the IRS.

Step Three: Select Your Attorney

Assuming your checklists helped you decide that you have a potential case, the final step is selecting your attorney. This stage is very important. The efforts by your attorney in presenting your case to the IRS can be a big factor as to how the agency attorneys perceive your case and whether it gets the attention it deserves. Again, you should choose an attorney based upon a combination of their legal ability and any personal attributes that are important to you.

As to ability, they must be able to properly evaluate your case, present a convincing application that meets all of the requirements of the statute, and work well with the government. Plan to ask them what prior DOJ Reward Program and what government contract experience they possess. As indicated above, the role of your attorney is heightened because the IRS is the one who determines if the public disclosure bar or original source exception applies. The IRS may be more willing to respond to a legal memorandum based upon legal research than if you act *pro se* or hire counsel unfamiliar with these complex standards. This is made even more important due to the fact that courts are divided on these standards.

With respect to personal qualities, this is a subjective determination made individually by each whistleblower. Be sure to hire an attorney you are comfortable interacting with. Ask yourself if you feel confident that they will keep you appropriately informed and treat you with the appropriate concern and care. You will be connected to them for several years, so select someone who matches your personality. After you have made your selection, put your trust in them. Although you can expect regular updates, don't be a pest. Reread this book to keep the long-term perspective in mind.

Step Four: Fill Out the Questionnaire

If you are serious about reporting tax fraud, you should be willing to answer a detailed questionnaire to provide your attorney with the facts he needs. Over the years, I have developed questionnaires and screening tools to help evaluate fraud cases. Many of the questions here will be asked of you later by your attorney. If you have taken the time to answer them at your leisure, it will be much easier to answer them in a live interview later. Below is a sample questionnaire for tax fraud.

As you consider how to answer these questions, be guided by these three principles:

1. Be truthful, without exaggerating
2. If you don't know or are not sure about something, say so
3. Provide as much detail as possible

For some of the more detailed questions about a tax evasion scheme or your evidence, plan to write several paragraphs. As discussed in Chapter Twenty-One, attorneys vary regarding whether they ask you to include the name of the company or individuals engaged in fraud at this stage. In any event, the primary purpose of this form is to allow your potential attorney to initially gauge the nature, size, and strength of your case. Your responses will facilitate any future discussion with your attorney. After they review your form, they will contact you for more details if they think you have a potential case and that they might represent you.

Confidential Questionnaire for Tax Fraud

1. Name, address, email address, and telephone number
2. Are the allegations that a "company" cheated on their taxes? (Yes or No)
3. Are the allegations that an "individual" cheated on their taxes? (Yes or No)
4. If the allegations are that an individual cheated on their taxes, did the person have at least $200,000 in income during one year? (Yes or No)
5. If the allegations are that an individual cheated on their taxes, did the person underpay taxes by a total of $2 million? (Yes or No)
6. How much money did the company or individual underpay on their taxes? (Describe how you calculated or estimated the amount)
7. Briefly explain the tax fraud allegations and why you believe they knew that they cheated
8. How did you become aware of the tax fraud?
9. Do you have any documents to help prove the tax fraud? (If so, briefly describe the type of documents)
10. When did the fraud occur? (Please state which years, when it stopped, and if it still going on)
11. If the allegations are against a "company," did you once work for the company committing the tax fraud? (Yes or No)
12. If the allegations are against a "company," do you now work for the company committing the fraud? (Yes or No)
13. Did you already tell the person or company that you thought they underpaid taxes? (If yes, briefly state what you did and how they responded; if no, don't talk to them about it until after you talk to an attorney)

14. Have your allegations been the subject of any legal action or newspaper story, or have the allegations been disclosed in any lawsuit, agency hearing, congressional hearing, or government audit? (If so, briefly describe them)

15. Have you talked to another attorney about this matter? (Yes or No)

16. Have you filed a lawsuit against anyone or a company before? (If yes, briefly describe them)

As discussed in Chapter Twenty-One, expect any law firm to ask you to acknowledge that filling out a questionnaire does not create an attorney-client relationship. A sample disclaimer used by attorneys is also included in that chapter.

Even though there is no formal attorney-client relationship, do not be hesitant in providing this information. As stated in Chapter Twenty-One, by law this information will remain confidential. In addition, your potential attorney needs this information to determine if he can represent you. Therefore, be frank and forthcoming.

CHAPTER THIRTY

To Use or Not to Use an Attorney

If there were no bad people, there would be no good lawyers.

— CHARLES DICKENS (1812–1870)

Unlike the DOJ program, you do not need to use an attorney to file for an IRS reward. This chapter discusses whether it is a good practice to ask an attorney to take your case on a contingency basis.

In the old IRS program, the help of attorneys was discouraged. As a result of excluding the use of legal representation, the IRS was able to act arbitrarily in deciding who to give awards to and what percentage to pay. As indicated previously, the amount of rewards to these unrepresented citizens was often less than two percent, and citizens had no way of knowing whether the IRS had simply used their information without paying their reward.

Today, however, the new IRS program allows the use of attorneys. This raises a new question about whether it is in the best interest of a person to file an application alone or grant an attorney a contingency fee when applying to the IRS Reward Program.

If there is value added by the attorney, then it makes economic sense for you to share the reward with an attorney. Actually, this is the same decisional framework the IRS faced when it decided whether to pay citizens rewards for reporting fraud in establishing the program. For the IRS, the cost-benefit analysis favored paying rewards, even though it meant giving up a share of the recovery.

In most cases, a cost-benefit analysis favors hiring experienced counsel as well. The value added is that an attorney, experienced with reward programs, will more likely prepare an application in a manner that appeals to the busy IRS workers trying to decide which cases warrant opening an investigation. If your attorney is highly respected, like those who specialize in DOJ fraud cases an IRS agent might be more willing to open an investigation in your case.

Remember, there is no appeal process if the IRS declines to open an investigation. The veteran attorney will be able to suggest to the IRS agent an investigative strategy that appears well reasoned and sound. They will also present the case in a manner that entices.

Imagine for a moment that you are an IRS agent. You have a stack of case files. You grab the top two. One is from a *pro se* individual (someone not represented by counsel) and the other is from a person represented by a former DOJ attorney with 15 years of experience uncovering fraud, who has recovered $1 billion in his career. Which case will you be more excited by?

Perhaps you are concerned that the *pro se* applicant has a vendetta or is paranoid, seeing fraud everywhere. On the other hand, you know that the former DOJ attorney has already screened this case before filing it with the IRS and he only presents those cases worthy of his name and reputation. A veteran attorney will also know how to estimate damages in a realistic manner, something appealing to the IRS.

An attorney can also add value by being an advocate for the whistleblower. Perhaps the IRS agent will be more willing to talk to an attorney who understands the process than an individual only wanting to know when they may get a reward. Thus, he can advocate directly to the IRS agent. The attorney can also assess whether the amount of any reward meets the statutory minimums and aid the agent in assessing which range of reward to use. Your attorney can also appeal to the tax court the level of a reward paid by the IRS. The agent knows the appeal process and may be more willing to negotiate a settlement with an attorney than a lay person if there is a grey area.

Importantly, your attorney also needs to do what he can to keep the IRS from placing you in the zero to ten percent range. An attorney familiar with the DOJ program will be well positioned to protect your interests in this regard. As indicated earlier, if the IRS contends that there was a public disclosure and you do not meet the original source exception, you fall in the zero to ten percent range.

The good news is that, unlike the DOJ program, the defendant is not the one raising this issue. That means that the defendant will not be enlisting high-priced attorneys making legal arguments why you are not eligible for a reward. It is something negotiated between you and the IRS. If you have counsel, they will be your advocate. They can even prepare a legal memorandum citing cases and court decisions from the DOJ Reward Program. This would be difficult for you to do on your own. You would be at the mercy of the IRS agent as to what range and how much you receive. In the years prior to the new program, this often meant the whistleblower received two to seven percent.

Finally, because the appeal rights available under the IRS Reward Program are expressly limited to filing a legal proceeding before the tax court, this step will require you to hire an attorney, even if you haven't been using one from the start. A lay person simply won't be expected to handle an appeal to a court *pro se*. Besides, what sense would it make to hire an attorney only after the IRS decides to reduce your award, rather than prevent it in the first place?

Attorney Fees

Expect to pay the same rate of contingency fees for using a quality attorney under this program as you would under the DOJ Reward Program, or roughly 40 percent. Because the IRS Reward Program does not allow your attorney to charge the defendant any additional fees, the only payment they receive is a portion of your reward. Preparing a solid IRS reward application is a tremendous risk for a quality attorney. Again, seasoned counsel will not simply fill out a form and ask you to sign an affidavit. If that is all the attorney you are considering using plans to do, forgo counsel, fill out your own form, and hold your breath.

Your attorney, if they understand the reward process, actually earns the reward by conducting legal research, gathering facts, and preparing a convincing application. They will also keep in regular communication and encourage the IRS to pursue the case. They become an extension of the IRS by creating an investigative plan and offering to assist in developing the case. In short, taking your case means forgoing working on cases paying by the hour. Attorneys really do take a monetary risk to handle this type of a case, so don't begrudge them their due.

In the end, whether to hire an attorney and which attorney to hire are subjective decisions each person must make for themselves. But they should be carefully thought through up front. I can't emphasize enough that there are no second chances when filing for these types of rewards.

The criteria I use when selecting cases and details regarding how to ask me to analyze your potential case are listed at the back of this book under *About the Author*. I also have additional information on selecting counsel on my website.

CHAPTER THIRTY-ONE
Revisiting the Case Study

Law is order and good law is good order.

— ARISTOTLE (384–322 BC)

I t is time to revisit the case study in this section. Now that you know more about the process, you will be able to look for the ways in which this hypothetical whistleblower met the *Four F Factors*. Doing this may help you better appreciate the IRS program in order to either submit a good application or keep you from wasting your time on a marginal matter.

Our case study began with a description of the whistleblower. Joanne was an employee of *DiamondsR4Now*, a company that was cheating, not only on federal income tax, but on state sales taxes as well. The scheme consisted of failing to ring up "cash" sales on the cash register. The company used the cash register receipts as the basis for declaring income, as well as state sales tax. But it failed to report sales based on cash, giving customers handwritten receipts for these purchases. In fact, buying and selling things for cash in order to avoid paying taxes is quite common, but it is difficult for the IRS to prove without help from an insider.

Joanne had firsthand knowledge that the company was cheating because her employer admitted it to her. To support her claim, she also made some copies of the handwritten cash receipts. The company kept these receipts for other business purposes, such as for customer records, as well as knowing the true sales volumes for inventory and other projecting purposes.

At first, Joanne was not sure what to do. She read this book and then contacted an attorney who was experienced in these types of cases. She sent him a completed questionnaire similar to the one in this book. Because the questionnaire was detailed, the attorney needed nothing more to make a determination that the claim appeared worth pursuing. He contacted Joanne and gathered some additional information.

Together, they were able to put together a convincing application to the IRS. In it, they explained in detail the nature of the fraud and provided an estimate of the amount of underpayment of taxes. Since Joanne knew approximately how much the company collected in income, she could estimate the underpayment. Her attorney did some additional research regarding trade shows, conducted legal research on the tax issues, and gathered public information about the company to provide a more complete picture of the company and alleged underpayments.

In addition, the attorney attached the documents Joanne had copied and explained their value. He even suggested an investigative game plan, identifying other potential witnesses and sources of documents. The application identified the names of the taxpayers, both the company and the individuals, in case the IRS was able to determine an amount over $2 million from the individuals.

Because the misconduct was in Washington, D.C., which has a reward statute, Joanne's attorney knew she was also eligible for a reward under the state *qui tam* statute. The company had not only failed to report income to the federal government, it had also failed to report state sales tax by concealing the cash sales. The state application, however, was different than for the IRS. An attorney would actually have had to file a complaint in federal court and allege fraud. Under the facts of the case, this was not a difficult hurdle. Furthermore, the owner admitted she was cheating.

Joanne's attorney prepared both the IRS application and the complaint to be filed in connection with the sales tax fraud. Both of the two final applications were compelling. Joanne read through it and gladly signed an affidavit stating that the information she provided was true to the best of her knowledge. She was pleased that the application stated the misconduct in such a clear, complete, and concise manner. After weighing the risks, she gave the green light to her attorney to submit both.

The attorney presented the application to the new IRS whistleblower office in Washington, D.C. He made sure that the IRS officials were aware that he was prepared to provide assistance on the case in whatever needs the agents might have. He also filed the state claim in the proper court and served the correct D.C. official to become eligible for a reward.

Parallel IRS and D.C. Investigations

One of the first things the IRS agent did after reading the application was to look at the tax returns of those alleged to have underpaid taxes. The IRS agent learned that the company had only reported $1 million in sales for the prior year. Based upon Joanne's information, the income was considerably more than that from estimates at trade shows alone, not taking into account sales from its store front. The agents were pleased that Joanne's attorney had provided some documentation, but they were most excited that they had a witness who could state that the company had intentionally failed to report income. The quote from the application was an eye catcher, "No records means no sales tax or income tax." This would meet the definition of fraud, which had a longer statute of limitations than simple underpayment of taxes. The agent gladly opened an investigation.

The D.C. government was also interested in the underreporting of sales tax. It was a significant and widespread problem. This case had good facts to support the allegations. In addition, the fact that the IRS was involved meant that it could combine its investigative resources to recover government funds.

One of the first steps was for the IRS to seize the company's books. It did not take long to determine that the company had underpaid taxes by several million dollars. The only difficulty with this case was that the wrongdoers did not have sufficient funds to pay the full extent of the fraud. As often happens, the company agrees to pay what it can afford. Here, it settled by paying $750,000 to the IRS and D.C. government. The owner of the store also pled guilty to a felony and was sentenced to 18 months in jail.

The issue of amount of a reward was next on the agenda. The IRS had initially argued that the amount recovered was under $2 million and, therefore, Joanne was not eligible. Her attorney, however, was a strong advocate. He had two legal positions. First, he sought to convince the IRS that this was fraud by a company, which did not have the $2 million threshold requirement. Although the IRS initially baulked, he convinced the IRS that the people buying jewelry were buying from a company, not an individual. In addition, he pointed out that even if the fraud was by an individual, the threshold is based upon the amount of fraud, not the actual recovery. Here, there was solid proof of more than $2 million in underpayments. The IRS agreed that she was eligible for a reward for one or both of these reasons, and that she fit within the 15 to 30 percent range.

The attorney also convinced the D.C. government that his client was entitled to a reward under its state reward statute. He filed the proper forms and showed how she met all of the requirements. The D.C. government agreed she fell within its 15 and 25 percent range.

For settlement purposes, the attorney for Joanne convinced both governments that a reasonable reward would be 18 percent of the $750,000 total. This was a great result for Joanne, which gave her $135,000 prior to taxes and the contingency fee to her attorney. Not only did she do the right thing, but her reward enables her to later attend law school to become an advocate for the disadvantaged, her lifetime dream.

Why It Worked

This is a classic case because the whistleblower had firsthand knowledge of the fraud. She had heard with her own ears that the company was underpaying federal taxes, as well as state sales tax. She also had some corroboration beyond her own words, namely, some documents from the company. It didn't matter that the documents were not smoking guns. It made her more credible and gave the governments more confidence that fraud really was afoot.

The fact that she used an experienced attorney was also a factor, as the applications were well written and clearly described the information most helpful to investigators. The amount of the fraud was not *de minimus* (i.e., an amount too small to consider worth the effort), which was a factor in the agent opening an investigation.

Although there was a moment where Joanne had to hold her breath when the IRS initially contested her eligibility, her attorney was skillful and persuasive without being obnoxious. He used his negotiating skills to work out a deal acceptable to everyone, an 18 percent reward.

If this case had not involved a company, there is a chance that the amount of recovery may not have met the $2 million minimum and there would not have been any IRS reward. The state fraud, however, would have been available regardless. Assuming that the amount of the settlement for the state fraud was one-third of the total, the state would have paid Joanne 18 percent of $250,000, or $45,000. The sales tax case, if standing alone, would be as small a case as you might expect an experienced attorney to accept. In fact, many attorneys would not take a $250,000 case. But her lawyer proved his worth.

Another Side to the Case Study

Even though the case study resulted in a happy ending, this type of fraud is very difficult to prove. It is not enough to merely know that a company is making cash sales. For instance, a company may sell fireworks or have a food stand at a county fair. These types of businesses regularly are cash and carry. Even if you believe they are not reporting all of the cash sales, proving it and the amount is another matter entirely. Not only must you show that they did not intend to pay taxes, but you must also have a valid means of quantifying it. This may require more than a hunch or even a general statement of admission by the owner.

In addition, don't lose sight of the fact that the amount of fraud is the amount of taxes owed, not the amount of income not reported. As indicated earlier, it would take $7 million in unreported income to equal $2 million in unpaid taxes.

Finally, the IRS will need to actually collect the back taxes. If the person hides their assets or spends the funds as quickly as they obtain them, don't expect the IRS to get excited about trying to confiscate a used boat or car to satisfy tax debts. Your reward will be based on the amount the IRS recovers. If the person owes $2 million in back taxes, but the IRS only recovers $50,000, your reward will be roughly 20 percent of $50,000 or $10,000. This helps explain why an attorney may not be excited about taking cases against individuals, especially when they are allegations that not all cash sales were reported.

Conclusion

There is no kind of dishonesty into which otherwise good people more easily and frequently fall than that of defrauding the government.

— BENJAMIN FRANKLIN (1706–1790)

As much as ten percent of all government spending goes to pay fraudulent bills. Similarly, ten percent of all federal taxes are underpaid. These figures amount to more than $200 billion in losses to the government each year. If these funds are not recouped from those who are cheating, that money will have to be made up by the remaining 90 percent of honest taxpayers.

The threat of government audits has lost it sting. The government lacks resources to conduct many audits, and it is widely known that less than two percent of Medicare filings and tax returns are audited. More and more people are finding that they can get away with cheating. These individuals and companies know that there simply are not enough government officials to guard the chicken coop.

A new strategy was needed. The government found it when it decided to reward private citizens for becoming watchdogs. Because a worker is worth his wages, the government has initiated reward programs where up to 30 percent of the funds recovered go to the one reporting the fraud.

Today, there are three different government reward programs that cover the bulk of the fraud being committed against the federal and state governments. These reward programs have set out welcome mats and issued warm invitations to citizens willing to partner with the government in fighting fraud. These reward programs allow the government to pay up to 30 percent of the funds recovered.

The programs easily could pay over $50 billion in rewards each year, if more good cases were filed by whistleblowers. Presently, the government is paying only a fraction of that in rewards each year. Clearly, there are many more opportunities for whistleblowers to receive rewards.

Under the DOJ program, the average reward is $1.75 million. As more citizens learn of these programs, the total amount of rewards will keep increasing.

All that glitters is not gold, however. It is important to know what type of case is eligible and how to assess whether your particular case is worth filing. It would cripple the government if thousands of people dashed off applications with little evidence and less hope of recovery. The risk would be that the program would be terminated and the government would lose the valuable contributions of the public.

That is why this book has two purposes. The first one is obviously to communicate the workings of the reward programs, so that you, as a member of the public, will know how to obtain the rewards Congress has authorized. Second, and equally important, is to describe the programs in sufficient detail that you will know when *not to file* for a reward. If your case is not worth reporting, it would be a shame for you to waste your time and distract the dedicated government workers who are trying to reclaim government funds.

I wish you the best in your efforts to report fraud and collect your reward! Keep in mind that my website will be regularly updated and expanded with additional resources to help you and all of those who are willing and able to stop fraud (www.HowToReportFraud.com).

Appendix

Conducting Your Own Research

Only the first whistleblower to file under the reward programs is entitled to a government reward. This is one of the *Four F Factors*, also known as First to File. (See Chapter Six.)

Needless to say, it is important to determine if another person has claimed a reward for the same fraud. Seasoned attorneys will conduct a quick search of public information to get a clue to whether your fraud allegations will be barred because they are not the first filing.

If the attorneys should learn that another whistleblower has already filed a suit, they will need to assess whether your entire claim is barred or whether some issues survive. It is possible that the first person to file only alleged a certain type of fraud or for a few years. For instance, the first person may have alleged that a hospital engaged in fraud by substituting a generic aspirin for a name brand and billed for the more expensive product. Your allegations might be that the person was not eligible for Medicare or that the hospital received a kickback from the pharmaceutical company. If your allegations include other types of fraud or a different time period, the first to file prohibition may not apply.

This aspect of evaluating your case is a critical point in time for making a decision whether to take your case and how to present it to the government. After all, nobody expects to receive a sizeable reward for reporting old news.

There is nothing magical about the way attorneys check for this information. In fact, you can conduct the same type of search yourself, which may keep you from wasting time and energy hiring a law firm to do it.

Suppose you work for King Pharmaceuticals (King) and you have reason to believe that the company concealed from the government its true "best prices" of certain drugs. (Although a real company is used here, it is not an implication that this pharmaceutical company is any better or worse than another, or that it is engaged in any misconduct. It is merely an illustration to show you how to examine SEC filings.) You are concerned that the company is underreporting the amount it owes to the government under the Medicaid Rebate Statute, as discussed in Chapter Seven.

There are two simple steps attorneys use to investigate prior reward claims. First, they examine what the defendant discloses on its own corporate website or in its Securities and Exchange (SEC) filings. If a company sells shares of stock, it must provide notice to potential shareholders of any known government investigations or lawsuits. Every quarter the company must submit a Form 10Q report to the SEC, and every year it must submit a Form 10K report. In both reports, the company must list a section for lawsuits or government investigations. It is simply a matter of reading the table of contents to locate where the company discloses this information.

Even though a whistleblower suit is filed under seal and the company may not know for sure that a whistleblower suit was filed, in practice the company often has enough information that it must list the allegations in its SEC reports. This is because the government usually contacts the company as part of evaluating each whistleblower suit. Although the government won't reveal that a whistleblower stepped forward, the government will be asking for information or documents. The mere fact that the government is asking questions is often enough to trigger a disclosure requirement.

It is fairly simple to navigate through a company's SEC filings in order to find details regarding government investigations or lawsuits.

One useful site is http://finance.yahoo.com. Near the top of the page is a link, entitled "Finance Search." Click on it, and then type in the name of the company, (i.e., King Pharmaceuticals). The website will then display a myriad of information regarding the company. For instance, it lists the symbol used by the stock exchange for the company (KG). If you click on this symbol, it will take you to a page that contains the SEC filings. There is a long list of links on the far left side of the page, one of which is "SEC Filings." When you click on that link, a list of filings will be shown. Select the most recent 10Q or 10K and click on it. (Note: The forms starting with the number 8 are special reports, often limited to a single topic. Unless they relate to announcing a fraud investigation, they normally do not contain relevant information.)

If you click on the March 1, 2007 "10K," you will be able to read the full SEC filing. Select the "Full Filing." Scroll down and find the table of contents, where you will find something similar to a link to "Legal Proceedings." When you click on the link, it takes you to the page where all of the legal proceedings are located. Often, a company will explain each lawsuit filed against it, followed by any government investigations.

When you get to the legal proceedings section, you will be told, "Please see Note 18 'Commitments and Contingencies' in Part IV, Item 15(a)(1), 'Exhibits and Financial Statement Schedules' for information regarding material legal proceedings in which we are involved."

Do not despair if you don't know how to find this section. You can scroll back to the Index at the beginning of the document and find a link to Part IV, Item 15. Click on Part IV.

Because you are told that the lawsuits are discussed at Note 18, scroll down in Part IV, until you find Note 18, entitled "Commitments and Contingencies" (a fancy way of listing things that could happen, *e.g.*, it could lose a lawsuit). A government investigation is listed as a contingency because payment is contingent upon it either settling or losing the allegations.

All that is left is a little bit of detective work.

There are several pages of descriptions of contingent items. Which are relevant? That depends on what allegations you are making.

Read the whole section. The first three sections discuss "Fen/Phen Litigation," "Thimerosal/Children's Vaccine Related Litigation," and "Hormone Replacement Therapy," which relate to product liability, not underpayment of Medicaid Rebates.

The next section is entitled, "Average Wholesale Price Litigation." Bingo. This section states that there are allegations the company "fraudulently inflated their average wholesale prices (AWP) and fraudulently failed to accurately report their 'best prices' and their average manufacturer's prices and failed to pay proper rebates pursuant to federal law." The report states that the allegations are from 1992 to the present.

From this information, there is a question whether your allegations are covered by this investigation. Isn't it better to find out early whether you have a good shot at a reward?

This is something you and your prospective attorney will need to discuss. He may want to contact the government and discuss whether you bring something new to the table and are eligible for a reward. Perhaps your allegations involve a different drug or a different scheme. Your best bet is to rely upon experienced counsel to navigate through the complex issues of First to File, as well as the Public Disclosure Bar.

The second method of checking on whether another whistleblower already filed a claim is conducting a simple Internet search. The search terms might look like this: "King Pharmaceuticals" or "best price" or "Medicaid Rebate." These three terms are likely to appear in an article discussing any investigations or settlements of these allegations.

One of the first search results is a press release by the Department of Justice, announcing that King agreed to pay DOJ $124 million to settle allegations that, between 1994 and 2002, it concealed its true best prices of all of its drugs sold to Medicaid. Based upon this information and scope of the release (*i.e.*, its entire line of drugs), it is doubtful that you could proceed with allegations of best price violations for conduct prior to 2002. However, if your allegations are that King was cheating after 2002, you would still need to continue your research.

You might also add to your search terms such as "false claims act" or "investigation" to narrow the results. Listing the name of the specific drug that was not properly reported could thin the list. It may take some detective work to weed through the myriad of hits, but it is often better to know up front whether you have been beaten out of a claim.

Of course, even if you suspect that another whistleblower has filed for a reward on a similar issue, you can always ask an attorney to confidentially evaluate your claims. Sometimes a second whistleblower has different or better information than the first and the two can join forces. An attorney experienced with the government reward programs can guide you through these issues.

A final reminder about conducting your own investigation; be mindful that if you talk too much to someone other than a potential lawyer, that person may use your information to file their own reward application. (See Chapter Six.)

Glossary

Carriers. Carriers are large for-profit companies — typically insurance companies, such as Blue Cross. The government hires Carriers or Fiscal Intermediaries (FIs) to administer the Medicare program. They make distributions of billions of dollars a year. They make initial decisions as to whether costs are allowable under the Medicare program. (See also Fiscal Intermediaries.)

Civil penalties. The False Claims Act allows the government to recover from a company that cheated under a government contract or program not only triple the amount of the fraud committed, but a civil penalty of between $5,500 and $11,000 per each false claim submitted. The initial text of the False Claims Act reads that penalties are to be between $5,000 to $10,000, but the statute was amended to automatically increase for inflation. It is now up to $11,000. The whistleblower is allowed to share as a reward for reporting fraud the amounts that the government recovers for both damages and civil penalties. (See also False Claims Act, *qui tam*, Whistleblower, Relator, Settlement, and DOJ Reward Program.)

Civil Fraud Section (aka DOJ Civil Frauds). A division of the Department of Justice in Washington, D.C., responsible for handling fraud and False Claims Act cases and overseeing the DOJ Reward Program. Generally, the Civil Fraud Section has responsibility for all fraud or False Claims Act cases over $1 million. Cases below that amount are within the primary authority of the United States Attorney's offices located throughout the United States. However, the United States Attorney often works jointly with the Civil Fraud Section on the larger cases. Conversely, the Civil Fraud Section frequently assists the United States Attorney with cases below this amount. In short, the two offices often combine efforts and make a formidable team. (See also DOJ Reward Program, United States Attorney.)

Complaint. This is the term used for the document used in filing a civil lawsuit. Under the DOJ Reward Program and state reward program, a whistleblower's attorney must file a complaint in district court alleging that the defendant has violated the False Claims Act by submitting false claims for payment under a government contract or program. (See also Decline, DOJ Reward Program, *qui tam*, Whistleblower.)

Decline to intervene. An option available to the DOJ when a *qui tam* lawsuit has been filed. Under the DOJ Reward Program and state reward program, the whistleblower files a civil lawsuit known as a *qui tam*. The civil action is filed "under seal," meaning that only the judge and the government sees the filing, not the defendant or the public. The False Claims Act statute grants the Department of Justice time to investigate the fraud allegations and make a decision whether to join and take over the *qui tam* lawsuit. The government will either "intervene" or "decline to intervene" in the case. If the government declines, the whistleblower has the opportunity to pursue the fraud case without the help of the government. The risks and rewards are heightened if they continue with a declined case. (See also Intervene, Complaint, DOJ Reward Program, *qui tam*, Whistleblower.)

Durable medical equipment devices (DME). Examples include motorized wheel chairs and pacemakers.

The Department of Justice (DOJ). The United States Department of Justice (DOJ) is a Cabinet department in the United States government. As part of the executive branch of the government, DOJ is the chief enforcer of federal laws and defender of the interests of the United States. Its roles include ensuring fair and impartial

administration of justice for all Americans. The DOJ is adminis-
tered by the United States Attorney General in Washington, D.C.,
together with the U.S. Attorneys located throughout the country.
There are many divisions and subsections of DOJ, one of which is
the Civil Fraud Section, which oversees and is primarily responsible for administering the federal whistleblower program under
the False Claims Act. (See also Civil Frauds, DOJ Reward Program,
U.S. Attorney's Offices.)

Department of Justice (DOJ) attorneys. The term used to describe
Civil Fraud Section attorneys and Assistant U.S. Attorneys assigned
to fraud cases. (See also Civil Frauds, DOJ Reward Program, United
States Attorney.)

Department of Justice (DOJ) Reward Program. This is the short-
hand way of describing the federal reward program under the False
Claims Act statute, which pays rewards to whistleblowers filing *qui
tam* complaints. (See also Complaint, False Claims Act, *qui tam*,
Whistleblower.

Discovery and Pre-Trial Practices. Generally, whenever a complaint
or lawsuit is filed, the parties are allowed to discover information in
the possession of other parties. Normally this includes the taking of
depositions (i.e., questions under oath in front of a court reporter
for possible use at trial) and asking for copies of documents relevant
to the case. When a whistleblower files a complaint in a False Claims
Act case under the DOJ Reward Program, the whistleblower is subject
to discovery, including being deposed. The whistleblower's attorney
is allowed to participate in discovery and protect the rights of the
whistleblower. (See also Complaint, *qui tam*, Whistleblower.)

False Claim. The False Claims Act statute generally prohibits a person
or company from knowingly presenting to the federal government
"a false or fraudulent claim" for payment. The statute states that the
term "knowingly" means that a person, with respect to information
"has actual knowledge of the information; acts in deliberate ignorance
of the truth or falsity of the information; or acts in reckless disregard

of the truth or falsity of the information." The statute also provides that no proof of specific intent to defraud is required. In short, a whistleblower does not need to prove actual fraud to show a false claim and be eligible for a reward. However, the standard is a fairly close cousin to fraud, and therefore it is often simplest to refer to a false claim as fraud. (See also False Claims Act, Fraud.)

False Claims Act (FCA). This is the name of the statute which, among other things, authorizes private citizens to apply for rewards for reporting fraud under the DOJ Reward Program. The statute can be found at 31 United States Code §§3729-3733. (See also Complaint, *qui tam*, Whistleblower.)

Food and Drug Administration (FDA). The federal government agency which approves the use of drugs and medical devices. If a company lies to obtain FDA approval, the sale of drugs or medical devices can amount to fraud under the DOJ Reward Program.

Freedom of Information Act (FOIA). A federal statute which allows any person the right to obtain documents held by federal agencies unless the records are protected from disclosure by an exemption in the law.

Federal Acquisition Regulation (FAR). This is a series of regulations issued by the federal government concerning the requirements of contractors for selling goods or services to the government. Most government agencies are required to use the FAR. The purpose of the FAR is to specify exactly how the government acquires products and services, including how to judge quality and price for items. It also spells out certain improper practices — such as kickbacks, undue influence, or corruption — that improperly influence purchasing decisions. Typically, when a government agency issues a contract, it will specify a list of FAR provisions that apply. A contractor must strictly follow all applicable FAR clauses contained in its contract. A knowing violation of a FAR clause could be the basis for a fraud action.

Fiscal Intermediaries (FIs). FIs are large for-profit companies hired by the government to administer the Medicare program. (See also Carriers.)

Fraud. Fraud is a generic term used to describe certain classes of misconduct. Broadly speaking, it is an intentional misrepresentation or a deception made for personal gain. The specific legal definition varies by jurisdiction, with some states requiring proof of each of as many as nine elements: (1) a representation; (2) falsity of the representation; (3) materiality of the representation; (4) speaker's knowledge of the falsity of the representation; (5) the speaker's intent which should be relied upon; (6) the hearer's ignorance of the falsity of the representation; (7) the hearer's reliance on the representation; (8) the hearer's right to rely on the representation; and (9) the hearer's consequent and proximate injury caused by reliance on the representation. In most civil lawsuits, the person alleging fraud must also provide clear and convincing evidence (a standard higher than in most civil cases) of the misconduct. The False Claims Act specifically states that a person does not need to prove fraud or actual intents to deceive to support a claim that someone submitted a false claim to the federal government. (See also False Claim, False Claims Act.)

Government Accountability Office (GAO). This is a non-partisan audit, evaluation, and investigative arm of Congress. The GAO was originally named the General Accounting Office. It is designed to "investigate, at the seat of government or elsewhere, all matters relating to the receipt, disbursement, and application of public funds, and shall make to the President ... and to Congress ... reports [and] recommendations looking to greater economy or efficiency in public expenditures."

General and Administrative (G&A) rates. These are allowable costs charged to the government, over and above the contract rate. When a company enters into with a government contract that pays for the costs incurred in performing work instead of a fixed price for delivering goods or services, it is allowed to bill the government certain G&A or overhead rates in addition to the amount paid to employees to cover the company's costs of running the plant. For instance, if a company has a contract to make tires for the government and is paid on a "cost" basis rather than $50 per tire, the company would bill the government the $20 per hour it pays the employee plus the G&A and overhead rates based upon certain formulas. The rules allow such costs as utilities and other costs of keeping the plant open. A company commits fraud when it includes into the rates costs not permitted under the rules, such as personal expenses or costs relating to a commercial contract.

Internal Revenue Service (IRS). The governmental agency responsible for collecting federal taxes and conducing audits relating to income tax filings. (See also IRS Reward Program.)

IRS Reward Program. Rather than relying almost exclusively upon audits, the IRS recently enacted a new whistleblower reward program paying 15 to 30 percent of the amount the IRS recovers in unpaid taxes based upon reports by citizens. It is modeled largely after the DOJ Reward Program.

IRS Form 1099. When a whistleblower receives a reward under one of the three government reward programs, the agency issues an IRS Form 1099 to the citizen. It is similar to a W2 issued to employees. The Form 1099 is also sent to the IRS. The whistleblower must claim the reward as income when filing annual income tax forms. (See also Whistleblower, *qui tam*, DOJ Reward Program.)

Intervene. An option available to the DOJ when a *qui tam* lawsuit has been filed. The False Claims Act statute grants the Department of Justice time to investigate the fraud allegations and make a decision whether to join and take over the *qui tam* lawsuit. The government will either "intervene" or "decline to intervene" in the case. (See also Decline, Complaint, DOJ Reward Program, *qui tam*, Whistleblower.)

Medicaid. Medicaid is the combined federal and state health insurance program for individuals and families with low incomes and resources. It is jointly funded by the federal and state governments. Each state manages the program within its borders. Examples of those eligible for Medicaid are low-income parents, children, seniors, and people with disabilities. Centers for Medicare & Medicaid Services monitors the program from the federal perspective. When a person or company cheats Medicaid, both the federal and state governments can bring actions to recover the funds. The government spends more than $250 billion for this program.

Medicare. Medicare is a federal government program which acts as a health insurance program. It covers people who are either age 65 and over, or who meet other special criteria. It was originally enacted on July 30, 1965. Currently, the federal government spends over $250 billion each year. Medicare is administered by the Centers for Medicare & Medicaid Services (CMS) [formerly HCFA], and hires carriers and fiscal intermediaries to run the program.

Public disclosure bar. Under the three government reward programs, the amount of a reward paid to a whistleblower will be eliminated or reduced if it is determined that the same information has already been publicly disclosed in the media or certain government reports. However, there is a significant exception to the public disclosure bar if the whistleblower's attorney can show that the whistleblower meets the definition of an "original source" of the information. The courts have not uniformly ruled upon what this exception means or when it applies and it is important for your attorney to be a strong advocate. Basically, if the whistleblower has firsthand knowledge of the fraud — perhaps due to the fact that he is an employee of the company that is cheating and has learned the information directly — he can satisfy the exception.

Qui tam (*qui tam* **lawsuit**). This term is derived from the Latin phrase, meaning "he who pursues a matter on behalf of the king, as well as for himself." (The most common pronunciation of the term *qui tam* is "kwee tom," but it is often sounded out as "key tam" or "kwee tam.") A person desiring to apply for a DOJ reward must file a civil lawsuit, which is often referred to as a *qui tam* lawsuit, as part of the application process. Generally, a person must hire a lawyer to file a *qui tam* lawsuit. Some courts have ruled that a *qui tam* lawsuit filed without being signed by an attorney must be dismissed and DOJ has never paid a significant reward to any person who did not use the services of an attorney to file a *qui tam* suit. (See also Complaint, DOJ Reward Program, Whistleblower.)

Relator. Not to be confused with a "realtor," who sells property, this term is the modern name for a whistleblower. It refers to the person filing a *qui tam* lawsuit under the DOJ Reward Program. The term "relator" is derived from the fact that the person is one who *relates* information to the government that fraud is afoot. (See also Whistleblower, *qui tam*, DOJ Reward Program.)

Settlement. This refers to when the parties reach a monetary settlement of a lawsuit or *qui tam* case. A whistleblower is allowed to share in the proceeds of settlements under all three government reward programs. (See also Complaint, DOJ Reward Program, *qui tam*.)

Statute of Limitations (SOL). The time within which a lawsuit must be filed or the right to file the lawsuit is lost. Under the DOJ Reward Program and state reward program, the SOL is a minimum of six years and is often lengthened to ten years, provided that the government acts within three years from when it learned of the fraud. The SOL for the IRS Reward Program is three years for simple mistakes and six years for other underpayment of taxes. But, there is no statute of limitation for tax evasion if you can prove fraudulent intent.

State reward program. Many states have adopted reward programs which mirror the DOJ Reward Program, with the primary difference being that it applies to fraud under state contracts and programs instead of fraud against the federal government. (See also Complaint, DOJ Reward Program, *qui tam*, Whistleblower.)

Three M's. This is the term the author uses to refer to the combination of Medicare, Medicaid, and the Military. They are three of the largest federal government programs.

U.S. Attorney's Offices. The United States Attorneys serve under the direction of the United States Attorney General of the Department of Justice (see Department of Justice). There are 93 United States Attorneys stationed throughout the United States and its territories. United States Attorneys are appointed by, and serve at the discretion of, the President of the United States, with advice and consent of the United States Senate. One United States Attorney is assigned to each of the judicial districts. The U.S Attorney is part of the Department of Justice. Each U.S. Attorney's Office has a team of Assistant United States Attorneys who handle criminal and civil actions on behalf of the United States for matters occurring within their jurisdiction either alone or jointly with Department of Justice attorneys from the main headquarters in Washington, D.C. They are also known as federal prosecutors. With respect to fraud or False Claims Act matters, the Civil Fraud Section of the Department of Justice in Washington, D.C. is primarily responsible for the DOJ Reward Program, but works closely with the U.S. Attorney's Offices on most cases. The False Claims Act requires a whistleblower to serve a copy of the *qui tam* complaint upon both the Civil Fraud Section and the local U.S. Attorney where the allegations occur. (See also Civil Fraud Section, Department of Justice, DOJ attorneys.)

Whistleblower. A whistleblower is someone willing to step forward and report fraud. It is often an employee who reveals wrongdoing within an organization to the public or to those in positions of authority. Unfortunately, the term whistleblower had often been viewed negatively. The three new government reward programs described in this book, however, extend the welcome mat by not using the term whistleblower. Rather, these reward programs use the name "relator" because the citizen *relates* allegations of fraud to and partners with the government in combating fraud against the government. (See also Whistleblower, DOJ Reward Program.)

About the Author

My name is Joel Hesch. I devoted over 15 years (1990 to 2006) as a trial attorney with the Civil Fraud Section of the Department of Justice (DOJ) in Washington, D.C. This is the office responsible for the modern-day DOJ Reward Program. My DOJ experience translates into over 25,000 hours directly analyzing and pursuing alleged fraud against 20 different federal agencies. I also personally worked on fraud cases resulting in over a billion dollars ($1,000,000,000.00) in judgments and recoveries, which paid more than $250 million in rewards to average citizens for reporting fraud. I was appointed to the DOJ Pharmaceutical Fraud Team and asked to testify on behalf of DOJ in a legal proceeding on the meaning and application of the False Claims Act's "Public Disclosure Bar" and "Original Source Exception."

When the then largest whistleblower case in history was being pursued, the Director of the Civil Fraud Section asked me to join a team of select DOJ attorneys. Together, we recovered a staggering $641 million from one company.

For my efforts, I received a Special Commendation Award for outstanding service. During my DOJ career, I also received a Meritorious Award and was twice bestowed the Special Achievement Award for sustained and superior performance of duty in combating fraud. In addition, I received certificate of appreciation from NASA for fighting fraud under the NASA Space Shuttle Program.

The director of the Civil Frauds Section made these statements in my work appraisals:

> *As has been true for many years, Mr. Hesch continues to show dedication to the office's mission of combating fraud and to working selflessly on whatever cases can best utilize his talents. We recognize and appreciate his fine efforts... Mr. Hesch is a delightful colleague and has the ability to work well on a team as well as independently... Joel has significantly exceeded expectations.*

At the end of fiscal year 2006, I left a rewarding career with DOJ to become a law school professor. I have written a scholarly law review article suggesting standards for the government and courts to follow regarding the "original source exception" within the DOJ Reward Program, which was cited five times in a brief to the United States Supreme Court. A copy of the article is located on my website.

I also am representing whistleblowers who are interested in reporting fraud under the DOJ Reward Program, various state reward programs, or the new IRS Reward Program. I engage the help of a team of hand-selected and experienced *qui tam* lawyers to assist me with my cases to ensure you and your case get the attention it deserves.

Mr. Hesch's Criteria for Accepting Cases

I have been asked to describe what criteria I use and how you can contact me to consider your case. As far as criteria, I am very selective in the cases I accept. There are two main reasons. First, my reputation matters. Each case I accept affects my reputation with the government officials reviewing the case. When I sign my name to an application on behalf of a whistleblower, I am attesting to the quality of the case being submitted. I have worked hard over the past two decades developing a good reputation and working relationship with the government officials overseeing government reward programs. I want them to look forward to receiving new applications bearing my name as counsel.

Second, the amount of a reward should be sufficient to outweigh the risks. Although I cannot guarantee results, I choose only those cases that I believe will be accepted by the government. I strictly follow my *Four F Factors* outlined in this book (see Chapter Six). Similarly, I only accept cases in which a significant reward is available.

This means that I do not accept a case where the loss to the government is less than $2 million. The reason for this threshold is simple. Because the reward will be roughly 20 percent of the amount the government recovers, a $2 million loss to the government equates to a potential reward of $400,000. This is before your attorney's share and taxes are deducted. I set an amount high enough so that at the end of the day, which is often more than two years later, both you and your attorneys feel like it was worth the effort. (If your case is under $2 million, my website contains information on locating attorneys that handle smaller cases).

How to Ask Mr. Hesch to Consider Your Case

If you think you have a case that meets my criteria and would like me and the attorneys I work with to confidentially examine your potential claim, you can either fill out the questionnaire form on line at my website (www.HowToReportFraud.com) or fax your answers to the questionnaires in Chapter Twenty-One for federal or state fraud or in Chapter 29 for IRS fraud to me at (866) 627-0076. When sending me this type of information, you understand that I follow the disclaimers listed in Chapter Twenty-One and the qualification that we have not agreed to represent you, but will use the information to make a determination whether you have a potential case and whether we will become your attorneys. After you submit your responses to the questionnaire, we will contact you. Be sure to provide me with an email address, as that is the manner in which I will initially respond to you.

I regret that I cannot respond to general questions about the reward programs or specific legal questions. I only consider taking cases when a person first fills out my questionnaire. Afterwards, we will contact you about your potential case.

Plan to visit my website for more updates and information regarding these exciting reward programs (www.HowToReportFraud.com).

Index

Additional Resources – How to Report Other Fraud

Credit Report Agency Errors/Fraud

The Federal Trade Commission (FTC) provides information for correcting errors on your credit report and how to obtain a free credit report. See http://www.ftc.gov/bcp/conline/pubs/credit/freereports.htm

Identity Theft

Each year 10 million Americans fall victim to identity theft, at a cost of $5 billion. The U.S. Post Office takes the lead on identity theft, and you can report it at: http://www.usps.com/postalinspectors/idthft_ncpw.htm

Immigration Fraud (Illegal Aliens)

To report an employer for knowingly hiring an illegal alien, contact the U.S. Immigration and Customs Enforcement toll free at 1-866-DHS-2-ICE. To report an illegal alien, contact the local immigration field office where the alien is located. See www.ice.gov. (Visit the author's website for a listing of telephone numbers organized by state.)

Internet Fraud

You may report fraud to the Internet Crime Complaint Center (IC3), a federal law enforcement agency, for possible criminal action at http://www.ic3.gov/

You should also report the fraud to your local state Attorney General's Office. (Visit the author's website for a listing of telephone numbers organized by state.)

Mail Fraud

To report mail fraud, contact the U.S. Post Office at: http://www.usps.com/postalinspectors/fraud/MailFraudComplaint.htm

Securities (Stocks) Fraud

To report investment fraud, contact the U.S. Securities and Exchange Commission (SEC) at: http://www.sec.gov/complaint.shtml

Other Resources from the Author

Updates to this book as well as helpful articles are contained on the author's website: **www.HowToReportFraud.com.**

Plan to sign up for his monthly newsletter, which provides practical tips on detecting and reporting fraud. The newsletters will also keep you informed on latest developments in the reward programs and government regulations addressing fraud.

(The author's biography is located on page 245.)